SERIOUS MONEY

CARYL CHURCHILL

The Royal Court Writers Series
published by Methuen
in association with the Royal Court Theatre

METHUEN'S NEW THEATRESCRIPTS

First published as a paperback original in 1987 by Methuen London Ltd,
11 New Fetter Lane, London EC4P 4EE and in the United States of America by
Methuen Inc, 29 West 35th Street, New York, NY 10001,
in association with the Royal Court Theatre
Reprinted 1988

Copyright © 1987 by Caryl Churchill
Futures Song by Ian Dury and Mickey Gallagher
Five More Glorious Years song by Ian Dury and Chaz Jankel
Cover artwork by Gerald Scarfe
Printed in Great Britain by Expression Printers Ltd, London N7

British Library Cataloguing in Publication Data

Churchill, Caryl
    Serious Money.———(The Royal Court writers series)
    I. Title   II. Series
    822'.94   PR6053. H786

    ISBN: 0-413-16660-0

Serious Money was first performed at the Royal Court Theatre, London, on 21 March 1987, with the following cast:

SCILLA TODD *a LIFFE dealer*	LESLEY MANVILLE
JAKE TODD *Scilla's brother, a commercial paper dealer*	JULIAN WADHAM
GRIMES *a gilts dealer*	GARY OLDMAN
ZACKERMAN *a banker with Klein Merrick*	ALFRED MOLINA
MERRISON *a banker, co-chief executive of Klein Merrick*	BURT CAESAR
DURKFELD *a trader, co-chief executive of Klein Merrick*	ALLAN CORDUNER
GREVILLE TODD *Jake and Scilla's father, a stockbroker*	ALLAN CORDUNER
FROSBY *a jobber*	JULIAN WADHAM
T.K. *personal assistant to Marylou Baines*	BURT CAESAR
MARYLOU BAINES *an American arbitrageur*	LINDA BASSETT
JACINTA CONDOR *a Peruvian businesswoman*	MEERA SYAL
NIGEL ABJIBALA *an importer from Ghana*	BURT CAESAR
BILLY CORMAN *a corporate raider*	GARY OLDMAN
MRS ETHERINGTON *a stockbroker*	LINDA BASSETT
DUCKETT *chairman of Albion*	ALLAN CORDUNER
MS BIDDULPH *a white knight*	LESLEY MANVILLE
DOLCIE STARR *a PR consultant*	LINDA BASSETT
GREVETT *a DTI inspector*	JULIAN WADHAM
SOAT *president of Missouri Gumballs*	ALLAN CORDUNER
GLEASON *a Cabinet Minister*	ALLAN CORDUNER

Other parts played by the Company and members of the Royal Court Young Peoples' Theatre.

KEYBOARDS	COLIN SELL

Director	Max Stafford-Clark
Designer	Peter Hartwell
Lighting Designer	Rick Fisher
Sound Designer	Christopher Shutt
Musical Director and Arranger	Colin Sell
Assistant Director	Hettie Macdonald
Stage Manager	Bo Barton

Futures song: words by Ian Dury, music by Micky Gallagher
Freedom song: words by Ian Dury, music by Chaz Jankel

The play includes a scene from *The Volunteers, or The Stockjobbers* by Thomas Shadwell, 1692.

Note on layout

A speech usually follows the one immediately before it BUT:

1) When one character starts speaking before the other has finished, the point of interruption is marked / .
e.g.   MARYLOU.
            Now Albion's share price has rocketed
            It's time we sold out and pocketed / the profit.
        TK.
            We could wait and see what Duckett's planning to do.

2) A character sometimes continues speaking right through another's speech:
e.g.   JAKE.
            No, it's just . . . I'm in a spot of bother with the authorities / but it's no problem,
                I'm sorting it
        SCILLA.
            What have you done?
        JAKE.
            out, it's more what the sorting might lead to /

3) Sometimes a speech follows on from a speech earlier than the one immediately before it, and continuity is marked*.
e.g.   BRIAN.
            How much would it cost to shoot her through the head? *
        TERRY.
            You can't get rid of your money in Crete.
            Hire every speedboat, drink till you pass out, eat
            Till you puke and you're still loaded with drachs.
        MARTIN. ⎫
        DAVE.   ⎬   Drach attack! drach attack!
        VINCE.
            Why's a clitoris like a filofax?
        DAVE and OTHERS.
            Every cunt's got one.
        BRIAN.
            *And he says five grand.
where 'shoot her through the head?' is the cue to 'You can't get rid' and 'And he says five grand.'

4) Superior numerals appear where several conversations overlap at the same time.
e.g.   DAVE.
            I've got a certain winner for the 3.30 if anyone's interested.[4]
        BRIAN.
            You haven't paid us yesterday's winnings yet.
        DAVE.
            Leave it out, Brian, I always pay you.
        KATHY.
            [4]Come on gilts. 2 at 4 the gilts.
where Kathy starts speaking as Dave finishes his first speech, but Brian and Dave continue their dialogue at the same time.

A scene from The Volunteers or The Stockjobbers by Thomas Shadwell.

HACKWELL, MRS HACKWELL, *and two jobbers.*

HACKWELL.
    Well, have ye been enquiring? What Patents are they
    soliciting for, and what Stocks to dispose of?

1ST JOBBER.
    Why in truth there is one thing liketh me well, it will go all over England.

MRS HACKWELL.
    What's that, I am resolved to be in it Husband.

1ST JOBBER.
    Why it is a Mouse-Trap, that will invite all mice in, nay rats too, whether they will or no:
    a whole share before the Patent is fifteen pound; after the Patent they will not take
    sixty: there is no family in England will be without 'em.

2ND JOBBER.
    I take it to be great Undertaking: but there is a Patent likewise on foot for one walking
    under Water, a share twenty pound.

MRS HACKWELL.
    That would have been of great use to carry messages under the ice this last frost, before
    it would bear.

HACKWELL.
    Look thee Lamb, between us, it's no matter whether it turns to use or not; the main end
    verily is to turn the penny in the way of stock jobbing, that's all.

1ST JOBBER.
    There is likewise one who will undertake to kill all fleas in all the families
        in England–

2ND JOBBER.
    There is likewise a Patent moved for, of bringing some Chinese Rope-Dancers over,
    the most exquisite in the world; considerable men have shares in it.

1ST JOBBER.
    But verily I question whether this be lawful or not?

HACKWELL.
    Look thee, brother, if it be to a good end and that we ourselves have no share in the
    vanity or wicked diversion thereof by beholding of it but only use it whereby we may
    turn the penny, always considered that it is like to take and the said Shares will sell well;
    and then we shall not care whether the aforesaid dancers come over or no.

2ND JOBBER.
    There is another Patent in agitation for flying; a great virtuoso undertakes to outfly any
    post horse five mile an hour, very good for expresses and intelligence.

MRS HACKWELL.
    May one have a share in him too?

2ND JOBBER.
Thou mayst.

HACKWELL.
Look ye Brethren, hye ye into the city and learn what ye can; we are to have a
Consultation at my house at four, to settle matters as to lowing and heightening of
Shares: Lamb, let's away, we shall be too late.

Three different dealing rooms simultaneously. All have screens and phones.

Shares – GREVILLE
Gilts – GRIMES *and* OTHERS
Paper – JAKE *and* OTHERS

Shares

GREVILLE (*on phone*).
It's quite a large placement and what we've done is taken them onto our own books,
one of the first deals of this kind we've done since Big Bang, yes . . . It's Unicorn Hotels,
whom of course you know, they've acquired a chain of hotels in Belgium, and the main
thing is they're a perfect mirror of their hotels here, 70 per cent business, 3 and 4 star.
They acquired them for sixteen million, the assets are in fact valued at eleven million
but that's historic and they're quite happy about that. The key to the deal is there's
considerable earnings enhancement. It was a private owner who got into trouble, not
bankrupt but a considerable squeeze on his assets, and they were able to get them
cheap. I can offer you a million shares, they're 63 to 4 in the market, I can let you have
them for 62½ net. At the moment the profits are fourteen million pretax which is
eleven million, the shares pay 4.14 with a multiple of 13.3. With the new hotels we
expect to see a profit of twenty million next year paying 5.03 with the multiple falling to
12, so it's very attractive. This is only the beginning of a major push into Europe.
Essentially the frontiers have been pushed back quite considerably.

The following is heard after the overlapping scenes finish:

I would show them to Joe in New York but it's only five in the morning. He's usually
quite yielding when he's in bed but I don't think he'd want to start a whole new story.

Gilts

GRIMES *and his* MATE *in gilts dealing room of Klein Merrick.*
SCILLA *on LIFFE floor. Each has two phones.*

GRIMES (*to* MATE).
I'm long on these bastards.

MATE (*to* GRIMES).
3's a nice sell. They'd be above the mark.

GRIMES (*on phone*).
Scilla? Sell at 3.

SCILLA (*on two phones. To floor*).
　　10 at 3. 10 at 3.
　　(*On phone 2.*)
　　That's March is it?

MATE (*phone*).
　　6 Bid.

GRIMES (*phone*).
　　What you doing tonight?

SCILLA (*to floor*).
　　4 for 10. 4 for 10. Are you looking at me?
　　4 for 10.

GRIMES (*phone*).
　　Scilla?

SCILLA (*phone 1*).
　　Yes, we sold them.

GRIMES (*phone*).
　　What you doing tonight?

SCILLA (*phone 1*).
　　Going out later – hang on.
　　(*Phone 2.*) 4 for 10 nothing doing. Will he go to 5?
　　(*To floor.*) 5 for 10! 5 for 10!

GRIMES (*phone 2*).
　　Bid 28 at the figure.

MATE (*to* GRIMES).
　　I'm only making a tick.

GRIMES (*to* MATE).
　　Leg out of it.

SCILLA (*phone*).
　　Grimes?

GRIMES (*to* MATE).
　　Futures are up.
　　(*Phone*) Champagne bar / at six?

MATE (*phone*).
　　Selling one at the figure.
　　(*To* GRIMES.) I'm lifting a leg.

SCILLA (*phone 2*).
　　We got you 10 for 5 bid, OK?
　　(*Phone 1.*) Yes, champagne bar at 6.
　　(*Puts down phone 1, answers phone 2 again.*) Yes?

GRIMES (*phone 2*).
　　Get off the fucking line, will you please?

MATE (*to* GRIMES).
　　01 bid, 01 offered.

SCILLA (*phone 2*).
> No, it's 5 bid at 6. I can't help you, I'm afraid.

GRIMES (*phone 1*).
> Is it a seller or a buyer?
> (*To* MATE.) He don't want to take us because he don't want to pay commission.

MATE (*phone 2*).
> Offered at 4. Thanks very much but nothing done.

GRIMES (*phone 2 to* SCILLA).
> 5 March at 28.
> (*To.*MATE.) What are we long of?

SCILLA (*phone 1*).
> No, it's gone to 29.

GRIMES (*to* MATE).
> 29 bid.
> (*Phone 2.*) All right, 9 for 5.

SCILLA (*to floor*).
> 9 for 5! 9 for 5! / Terry!

MATE (*phone 1*).
> You'd better keep up, I'll be off in a minute.

GRIMES (*phone 1*).
> I'll make you a price, what do you want to do?

MATE (*to* GRIMES).
> Bid 4.
> (*Phone 1.*) I'm off, I'm off.

GRIMES (*to* MATE).
> They was offered at 4.
> (*Phone 1.*) Bid 3.

SCILLA (*phone 2*).
> Three month sterling opened at 89.27 for March delivery and they've been trading in a 4 tick range.

MATE (*phone 2*).
> Can't help you.
> (*to* GRIMES.) There's a fucking seller trying to make us pay up.

GRIMES (*phone 2*).
> Bid 3.

MATE (*to* GRIMES).
> I think we should buy them.

GRIMES (*phone 1*).
> Bid 4, bid 4 at 6.

SCILLA (*phone 2*).
> No, it's quite quiet.
> (*Phone 1.*) 9 for 5 a deal.

GRIMES.
> You're getting good at this. Extra poo tonight.

MATE (*phone 1*).
   2 bid at 5.
   (*To* GRIMES.) Am I still cheap?

GRIMES (*to* MATE).
   Sold 5 for 9 bid.

SCILLA (*phone 2*).
   Looks as if they may finish at 25.

MATE (*to* GRIMES).
   What shall we do overnight?

GRIMES (*to* MATE).
   I'll be long.

MATE (*to* GRIMES).
   You don't want to be too long.

GRIMES (*phone 2*).
   Closing out now at 4.

   GRIMES *starts going down a list on a piece of paper marking prices.*

MATE (*to* GRIMES).
   Doing the long end?

GRIMES (*to* MATE).
   How shall I mark these, 2 or 3?

MATE (*to* GRIMES).
   3.

GRIMES (*to* MATE).
   Does it make a lot of difference to you?

MATE (*to* GRIMES).
   Hundred thousand.

GRIMES (*to* MATE).
   You must have made that trading in the last half hour.

SCILLA (*to floor*).
   If you've lost any cards, Dave, I'm not helping you.

Paper.

JAKE *and another dealer sitting side by side. Two salespeople who shout from behind. Loud. American sound though they're not.*

SALES 1.
   I tell you what else here. Sweden / just called.

SALES 2.
   If you want to jump on the Hambro / bandwagon you better hurry.

JAKE (*phone*).
   We also have two Japanese. I'll make those 88 6.

SALES 1.
Sweden first 10 has been called. How do we go these days?

DEALER (*phone*).
There's also an issue coming out again.

SALES 2.
The new BFC for World Bank.

DEALER (*to* JAKE).
I've just sold some paper / like that.

SALES 1 (*phone*).
They're not taking. I'll give you a level.

DEALER (*to* JAKE).
Shall we go ahead?

JAKE (*to* DEALER).
Let's wait a few / minutes before we have the whole world crashing down on us.

SALES 2.
Chase Corporation 68 88.
He can bash you in with one arm. He's got a black belt in karate.

SALES 1.
He's a very nice guy.

JAKE (*phone*).
What I suggested was swapping into something longer, threes or whatever.

DEALER (*phone*).
I've been talking to Hong Kong.

JAKE (*phone*).
Because / it's up to 14.

SALES 1.
We're waiting on the Bundesbank here.

JAKE(*phone*).
He doesn't care at the moment, / David.

SALES 2.
Paris intervention rate / still at 8%. Buy 10.

DEALER (*phone*).
It's done.

JAKE (*phone*).
Band two are at thirteen-sixteenths. It's a softer tone today.

DEALER (to JAKE).
He just said to me 590, I said it's done. He would have said 610 wouldn't he?

JAKE (*to* DEALER).
Get back on.

SALES 1.
We have Frankfurt here, Frankfurt, guys.
Discount rate remains 3%. Lombard 5. Buy twos / twos, twos, twos.

DEALER (*phone*).
He said to me 595 . . . OK that would be great.

SALES 2.
Tokyo one month 4.28125.*

DEALER (*phone*).
Discretion is my middle name. Tell me tell me tell me tell me . . . you said you were going to tell me after lunch . . . / What, you bought some? . . . It's

SALES 1.
He broke an arm arm wrestling with a treasury bond dealer

DEALER.
going down . . . How fast do you want it to go down? . . . You're in profit, / it's 7-8 right.

JAKE (*phone*).
Listen, guy. Listen listen listen listen listen.
Lombard Intervention steady at 5.

DEALER.
It if takes at 6 . . . no it's not going to take at 5 . . . if it goes to 7 . . . You're such a sleaze, you're not really a man of honour, you said you'd tell me after lunch . . . / I didn't know that's

SALES 2.
The guy dealt with Citibank but got back to them too late.

DEALER.
What your best was . . . tell me tell me . . . Futures are crashing off.

JAKE (*phone*).
The Mori poll put the Tories four up.

SALES 1.
We're going to lose power any minute, that's official.

DEALER.
What the fuck?

JAKE (*phone*).
So the three month interbank sterling rate – no it's a tick under –

SALES 1.
We have Milan three months 11½.

JAKE (*phone*).
There's a discrepancy between band 2 and band 3 . . . I thought it might give us some arbitrage possibilities.

DEALER (*phone*).
Come on come on come on guy.

SALES 1.
What's with the ECU linked deposits for Nomura?

SALES 2.
Now hurry hurry hurry guys hurry.

Power goes – no screens, no phones.
Outcry.

JAKE.
Marvellous.

DEALER.
If the market moves in a big way we'll get cremated.

JAKE.
They left us a whole lot of orders we're meant to be filling.

DEALER.
I have to speak to Zurich.

SALES 2.
So what happens now?

SALES 1.
They go elsewhere, bozo.

Liffe Champagne Bar

SCILLA, *(trader with Liffe)* her brother JAKE *(commercial paper dealer)*, GRIMES *(gilts dealer) drinking together in the champagne bar.*

GRIMES.
Offered me sixty right? So next day
The other lot seventy five. OK,
So I go to the boss and go 'I don't want to trouble
You', and he goes 'All right you cunt,
Don't mess about, how much do you want?'
So I go – I mean why not – I go 'Double
What I'm getting now', and he goes 'fuck off'. Meanwhile
Zackerman rings and – this'll make you smile –
He goes, he goes, I'll give you a hundred grand,
Plus the car and that, and fifty in your hand,
But no thinking about it, no calling back,
This is my first and last. I say, Zac,
A good dealer don't need time to think.
So there you go. Have another drink.

JAKE.
So there's twenty seven firms dealing gilts.

SCILLA.
Where there used to be two.

GRIMES.
Half the bastards don't know what to do.

JAKE.
Those of you that do have got it made.

SCILLA.
And all twenty seven want ten per cent of the trade.

GRIMES.
So naturally there's going to be blood spilt.

JAKE.
>Ten per cent? Go in there and get fifty.

SCILLA.
>Everyone thinks it's Christmas and it's great to know they love you,
>But you mustn't forget there's plenty still above you.
>(There's at least two dozen people in the City now getting a million a year.)
>Think of the ones at the top who can afford
>To pay us to make them money, and they're on the board.

GRIMES.
>They're for the chop.

JAKE (*simultaneously*).
>I'm on the board.

SCILLA.
>   True, you're on the board,
>But how many of us will make it to the top?
>If we've a Porsche in the garage and champagne in the glass
>We don't notice there's a lot of power still held by men of daddy's class.

GRIMES.
>No but most of them got no feel
>For the market. Jake's the only public schoolboy what can really deal.

JAKE.
>That's because I didn't go to university and learn to think twice.

SCILLA.
>Yes, but they regard us as the SAS.
>They send us in to smash the place up and get them out of a mess.

GRIMES.
>Listen, do you want my advice?

SCILLA.
>They'll have us on the scrap heap at thirty five,

JAKE.
>I've no intention of working after I'm thirty.

SCILLA.
>Unless we're really determined to survive
>   (which I am)

JAKE.
>It probably means you have to fight dirty.

GRIMES.
>Listen, Nomura's recruiting a whole lot of Sloanes.
>Customers like to hear them on the phones
>Because it don't sound Japanese.
>If you want to get in somewhere big –

SCILLA.
>   Grimes, don't be such a sleaze.
>Daddy could have got me in at the back door
>But you know I'd rather be working on the floor.
>I love it down with the oiks, it's more exciting.

JAKE.
> When Scilla was little she always enjoyed fighting
> > (better at it than me.)

SCILLA.
> But it's time to go it alone and be a local.
> I'm tired of making money for other people.

GRIMES.
> (Going to make a million a year?

SCILLA.
> I might do.)

GRIMES.
> I tell you what though, Zackerman can recruit
> The very best because he's got the loot.

JAKE.
> I told him for what he's getting from my team, why be a meanie,
> He got rid of the BMW's and got us each a Lamborghini.
> He's quite a useful guy to have as a friend.
> So I thought I'd ask him home for the weekend.
> But I've got to go to Frankfurt Friday night,
> So Scilla, you can drive him down, all right?

SCILLA.
> I'm beginning to find Zackerman quite impressive.
> > (I wonder how he got to where he is now?)

GRIMES.
> My school reports used to say I was too aggressive
> > (but it's come in quite useful.)
> My old headmaster wouldn't call me a fool again.
> I got a transfer fee like a footballer. He thought I was a hooligan.
> He goes, you fool boy, you're never going to get to work,
> What use is a CSE in metalwork?
> I could kiss his boots the day he kicked me out of school.

> GRIMES *and* SCILLA *leave.*
> ZAC *enters.*

ZAC.
> So cut the nostalgia. I'm the guy they're talking about, Zac.
> I'm here for my bank, Klein Merrick, to buy up jobbers and brokers.
> And turn the best of them into new market makers.
> The first time I realised how fast things were changing was something that happened at
> > Klein's in New York a few years back.

MERRISON, *a banker, co-chief executive officer of Klein Merrick.*
DURKFELD, *a trader, co-chief executive officer of Klein Merrick.*

MERRISON.
So I told them 83 was a great year,
Profits up ten million on 82.
But we can do better than that by far.
Leveraged buyouts are the way to go
     (I told them).
Take Krafft, put up three million to acquire Hoffman Clocks,
Borrowed the rest of the fifty million, a year later makes a public offering, and pockets
     a whole fifty million plus he retains thirty million of stock.
That's eighty million dollars on his initial three.
And that's from taking a risk instead of a fee.
We advise other people on acquisitions.
They make the serious money. Fuck it all.
The company should take its own positions.
Partners should be willing to risk their own capital.
I told them, man is a gambling animal.
Risk is one of our company traditions.
Old Benny Klein took risks, the latest news
Meant profit, they'd say on Wall Street 'Let the Jews
Have that one,' and he would. Imagine the scene,
Guy comes and says 'I can make flying machines.'
Benny puts up the money, doesn't bat an eye,
He says, 'OK, so make the machines fly.'
When I was working with Henry under Nixon

DURKFELD.
Jack, I heard this speech before.

MERRISON.
There were quite a few things needed fixing –

DURKFELD.
Jack, I heard it already.

MERRISON.
So, I'm a bore.
Tell me, do you have a problem, Eddie?
I trust you've no more trouble with your wife?
It's a while since you took a good vacation.
None of us gets enough relaxation
     (I never even make it upstairs to the gym get a massage.)
Tell me what you want out of life.

DURKFELD.
I'm a simple guy, Jack. I walk in the woods
And shoot things. I don't talk so good
As you, I'm good on my own, I shoot straight,
I don't say, 'Shall I, shan't I?' You guys deliberate
One hell of a lot. I walk on my own
And I know I could run this show on my own.

MERRISON.
I'm not sure I understand what you're saying.

DURKFELD.
    I don't have the same alternatives
    A guy like you does. You say Henry
    Where I say Kissinger. You want to move?
    You've talked about some possibility.
    For me, this is enough.
    I don't look beyond this company.
    You ready to go do that stuff?

MERRISON.
    Let me understand what you're saying here.

DURKFELD.
    I want to go solo running Klein.
    I'm saying I'm suggesting you resign.

MERRISON.
    I just promoted you.

DURKFELD.
    Should I be grateful?

MERRISON.
    I made you my equal.

DURKFELD.
    Jack. I hate you.
    Didn't you know that? You're not so smart.
    You're too important to smell your own fart.

MERRISON.
    Eddie. I need to understand your problem.

DURKFELD.
    There's guys don't want me in their club.
    I don't give a rat's ass.
    Those guys would have looked the other way
    And let the cattle trucks pass.
        (I don't want to play golf with those bastards. I don't even play golf. I can walk
        without hitting a ball.)
    I'm good at my job.
    I stay on the floor with the guys.
    Screw the panelling, screw the Picassos, I am not interested in office size.
        (You like lunch, you have lunch.)
    I run the best trading floor in New York City,
    And traders make two dollars profit for this company
        for every dollar made by you bankers.
    And you treat us like a load of shit.
    You make me your equal, I'm meant to say thanks
    For that? Thanks, Jack. Come off it.
    I make this company eighty million dollars and bankers pocket most of that profit.
    Bankers get on the cover of Time.

MERRISON.
    Brother, can you spare a dime?

DURKFELD.
>I do OK, sure, I'm not talking greed.
>I'm talking how I mean to succeed.
>>(My father came to this country – forget it.)
>Which of us does this company need?
>I'm talking about indispensable.

MERRISON.
>And my father? You think I'm some kind of patrician?
>I was sweeping floors in my uncle's delicatessen
>So don't –
>The company needs us both. Be sensible.
>There's two aspects to the institution.
>Nobody means to imply they underestimate your invaluable contribution.
>I need to understand what you're saying here so let's set a time we can have a further
>>talk.

DURKFELD.
>You don't seem to get it. You're sitting in my chair. Walk.

ZAC.
>And the guy walked.
>>(He walked with twenty million dollars but he walked.)

>The financial world won't be the same again
>Because the traders are coming down the fast lane.
>They don't even know it themselves, they're into fucking or getting a Porsche, getting a
>>Porsche *and* a Mercedes Benz.
>But you can't drive two cars at once.
>If you're making the firm ten million you want a piece of the action.
>You know you've got it made the day you're offered stock options.
>There are guys that blow out, sure, stick too much whitener up their nose.
>Guy over forty's got any sense he takes his golden handshake and goes.
>Because the new guys are hungrier and hornier,
>They're Jews from the Bronx and spivs from South California.
>It's like Darwin says, survival of the fit,

>Now, here in England, it's just beginning to hit.

>The British Empire was a cartel.
>England could buy whatever it wanted cheap
>And make a profit on what it made to sell.
>The empire's gone but the City of London keeps
>On running like a cartoon cat off a cliff – bang.
>That's your Big Bang.
>End of the City cartel.
>Swell.
>England's been fucking the world with interest but now it's a different scene.
>I don't mind bending over and greasing my ass but I sure ain't using my own vaseline.

>Now as a place to live, England's swell
>Tokyo treats me like a slave, New York tries to kill me, Hong Kong
>I have to turn a blind eye to the suffering and I feel wrong.
>London, I go to the theatre, I don't get mugged, I have classy friends,
>And I go see them in the country at the weekends.

The meet of a hunt. On horses are ZAC, GREVILLE, *50, stockbroker, his daughter*
SCILLA, *and other hunt members, e.g.,* MRS CARRUTHERS, LADY VERE, MAJOR
and FARMER. FROSBY, *jobber, comes in late, on foot to watch.*

MRS CARRUTHERS.
    The hound that I walked goes up front with the best.

FARMER.
    The best of the pack is that cunning old bitch.

LADY VERE.
    His fetlocks swell up so I'll give him a rest.

MAJOR.
    Went over his neck and headfirst in the ditch.

GREVILLE.
    Stand still will you dammit, whatever's the matter?

MAJOR.
    Bottle of sherry he won in a raffle.

LADY VERE.
    Hunt saboteurs made a terrible clatter.

MRS CARRUTHERS.
    You can't hold her, Greville, in only a snaffle.

FARMER.
    It's colder today but the going's much quicker

SCILLA.
    Jumped onto the lawn and straight over the vicar.

GREVILLE.
    Good morning

MAJOR.
                    Good morning

GREVILLE.
                        Good morning

MRS CARRUTHERS.
                            Hello

GREVILLE.
    Good morning

LADY VERE.
                    Good morning

GREVILLE.
                        I don't think you know
    Mr Zackerman here, my colleague and guest.

MRS CARRUTHERS.
    The hound that I walked goes up front with the best.

GREVILLE.
    Mr Zackerman wanted to join us of course
    And Mrs Carruthers provided a horse.

MRS CARRUTHERS.
>He's terribly clever, won't put a foot wrong,
>When he hears the horn blow he'll be off like a rocket.
>His mouth's rather hard and he is very strong,
>Don't fight him, he'll pull out your arms by the socket.
>There's not a horse safer and not a horse faster,
>So don't step on hounds and don't override master.

LADY VERE.
>Making the most of the beautiful weather.

GREVILLE.
>American fellow, a friend of my daughter,
>Colleague of mine, we'll be working together.

SCILLA.
>Left behind at the gate and came off in the water.

FARMER.
>The best of the pack is that cunning old bitch.

MAJOR.
>Went over his neck and headfirst in the ditch.

LADY VERE.
>Hunt saboteurs made a terrible clatter.

GREVILLE.
>Stand still will you dammit, whatever's the matter?
>Priscilla insists upon working for Liffe.
>I was terribly doubtful and so was my wife.
>>(The London International Financial Futures Exchange,terrible place, full of the most frightful yobs)
>Hardly the spot for a daughter of mine
>But she buys her own horses and takes her own line.

LADY VERE.
>We've lost our head gardener, bit of a chore.

MAJOR.
>I'm sure Mr Zimmerman's hunted before.

ZAC.
>Not a great deal but I have been out a few times in Ireland with the Galway Blazers.

LADY VERE.
>In that case I'm sure you can give us a lead.

MRS CARRUTHERS.
>The girl's putting far too much oats in his feed.

SCILLA.
>Is is true?

ZAC.
>>Well I saw both the start and the finish.
>I was on foot drinking plenty of Guinness.

SCILLA.
>There aren't any gates and I'm not waiting for you.

ZAC.
You're so tenderhearted, that's why I adore you.

FARMER.
It's colder today but the going's much quicker

SCILLA.
Jumped onto the lawn and straight over the vicar.
    (So Klein have taken over Daddy. How long will he last? Five years?)

ZAC.
(He could be lucky.)

GREVILLE.
Not joining us Frosby? Find horses a bore?

MRS CARRUTHERS.
He's terribly clever, won't put a foot wrong.

LADY VERE.
We've lost our head gardener, bit of a chore.

CARRUTHERS.
His mouth's rather hard and he is very strong.

FROSBY.
I like a stroll to see the meet.
I'm happier on my own two feet.
Is that chap there the American?

GREVILLE.
Yes, it's Klein's Zac Zackerman.

FROSBY (*to himself*).
Yanks go home. Yanks are robbers.

GREVILLE.
Zac, I want you to meet a colleague I've done a great deal of business with over the
years, one of the jobbers,
Mr Frosby, Mr Zackerman.

ZAC.
Hi Mr Frosby, I can't really talk.
This horse won't stand still and he won't even walk.

MRS CARRUTHERS.
When he hears the horn blow he'll be off like a rocket.
Don't fight him, he'll pull out your arms by the socket.

GREVILLE.
No more long lunches for me, Frosby, no more lying in bed.
It's up at six now in the godforsaken
Dark cold mornings. On the bright side
The company does an excellent egg and bacon.

FROSBY.
Some things change, some things don't end.
After all, a friend's a friend.

MRS CARRUTHERS.
So don't step on hounds and don't override master.

ZAC.
Is this horse going to do what I tell it Priscilla?

MRS CARRUTHERS.
There's not a horse safer and not a horse faster.

SCILLA.
It's generally known around here as a killer.

ZAC.
(When I end up in bed with a broken leg I only hope you're going to look after me.)

SCILLA.
(Drop dead, bozo.)

The horn blows.
They all go in a rush, leaving FROSBY *alone.*

FROSBY.
The stock exchange was a village street.
You strolled about and met your friends.
Now we never seem to meet.
I don't get asked much at weekends.

Everyone had a special name.
We really had a sense of humour.
And everybody played the game.
You learned a thing or two from rumour.

Since Big Bang the floor is bare,
They deal in offices on screens.
But if the chap's not really there
You can't be certain what he means.

I've been asked to retire early.
The firm's not doing awfully well.
I quite enjoy the hurly burly.
Sitting alone at home is hell.

I can't forgive Greville. He's gone with that Yankee bank buying it's way in, that Yak, Whack, whatsisname, Zac, trying to keep up with his children. His son Jake's one of these so-called marketmakers. Some of us have been making markets for thirty years. And his daughter Scilla works with those barrow boys in Liffe you'd expect to see on a street corner selling Christmas paper and cheap watches, they earn more than I do, they won't last.

I have a constant funny ache,
I can't see straight because of grief.
I really think my heart will break.
Revenge would give me some relief.

So now I'll phone the DTI,
Who want a clean and honest City.
Jake's no better than a thief
And why should I have any pity?
I've cried and now my friends can cry.

I've had the odd tip from Greville, I know he gets it from Jake and there's far more than
I ever see. Let the DTI investigate. The City's not mine any more so let it fall.

I love the masters in their pink
I'm glad traditions still exist.
I think I'll go and have a drink.
I love the valley in the mist.
    (I'm very frightened.)

    ZAC *phones* TK *and* MARYLOU BAINES *in New York.*

TK.
    This is Marylou Baines' personal assistant.

ZAC.
    It's Zac, I've got to speak to her this instant.
    I know it's 3 a.m your time, but I know she's awake.
    Tell her it's about Jake.

TK.
    Hi, Zac, this is TK here. Can I help you? What's the problem? Is it urgent?

ZAC.
    Stop talking like a tubful of detergent / .
    I got to speak to her now and not now but five minutes ago.

MARYLOU.
    Zac, is there something I should know?

ZAC.
    Jake's dead. They think it's suicide.

MARYLOU.
                       Thank you, Zac.
    Jake was a nice guy but I haven't heard from him since some time back.

She hangs up and speaks to TK

MARYLOU.
    Put anything from Jake Todd in the shredder.

    ZAC *phones* JACINTA CONDOR *in London.*

ZAC.
    Jacinta, it's me. / Bad news. Jake's been found shot. /
    It looks like suicide because he was in some kind of trouble with the DTI / though so far
       nobody seems to know exactly what.

JACINTA.
    Zac! What? My God.
    He was the English colleague I like the most (except for you.)
    I hope I never meet his unhappy ghost.
    I look forward to meeting. /

    JACINTA *phones* NIGEL AJIBALA.

JACINTA.
    Nigel, have you read the newspapers today?

NIGEL.
> No, what's the matter?

JACINTA.
> Don't panic, OK?

This overlaps with CORMAN *phoning* ZAC.

CORMAN.
> Zac, have you seen the fucking *Times* this morning?
> Why didn't Todd give us any warning.
> Why didn't he tell us about the DTI?
> Do you think he's talked?

ZAC.
> Deny. Deny. Deny.
> (Let them see what they can prove.)

This overlaps with JACINTA *phoning* MARYLOU.

JACINTA.
> Marylou, the delivery. You think we should wait a week?

MARYLOU.
> Hold off for twenty-four hours, OK? We'll speak.

NIGEL *phones* CORMAN.

NIGEL.
> Mr Corman, I'm deeply shocked that anyone associated with your company should be touched by the slightest breath / of scandal.

CORMAN.
> The deal's in no way affected by his death.
> (The deal is the priority.)

This overlaps with MARYLOU *phoning* ZAC.

MARYLOU.
> Zac, your news is causing a certain amount of tension.

ZAC.
> Can we still rely / on you?

MARYLOU.
> Sure, but never mention.

CORMAN *phones* MARYLOU *and gets* TK *on answering machine.*

CORMAN.
> TK? Marylou?

TK (*on machine*).
> Hello, this is the office of Marylou Baines. I'm afraid Ms Baines is not available right now to come to the phone,
> But if you wish to leave a message for her or for TK, her personal assistant, please speak for as long as you wish after the tone.

CORMAN.
> Fuck.

ZAC.

I went with Scilla to identify her brother Jake's body which was kind of a mess.

Then we stopped off for coffee, which was making me late for work, but it was a special occasion, I guess.

It'd be good if we could handle this

So you don't get associated with anything too scandalous.

(Just stick to No comment, and let them make things up.)

SCILLA.

Zac, I told the police I had breakfast with Jake at Klein Merrick yesterday morning. Just to say hello. But in fact he gave me a warning.

ZAC.

They know the DTI paid him a visit.

SCILLA.

But it wasn't just that. He was frightened of . . .

ZACKERMAN.

Well, what is it?

SCILLA.

What was Jake like? charming, clever, idle.

He won, he lost, he cheated a bit, he treated it all as a game.

Can you really imagine him killing himself for shame?

(He didn't know what honour meant.)

He wasn't telling me he was suicidal,

He was telling me . . . You may think it's absurd, but

I'm certain he must have been murdered.

JAKE *and* SCILLA *at breakfast.*

JAKE.

Don't let me worry you, I'm probably imagining it.

SCILLA.

Have you shared a needle?

JAKE.

Not Aids, I'm perfectly / healthy.

SCILLA.

At work they ask for tea in an Aids cup, they mean / a disposable because the dishwasher

JAKE.

Listen, I've a problem. Listen.

SCILLA.

What?

JAKE.

No, never mind, you know I left my diary at your place last week? / You haven't got it on you?

SCILLA.
>Yes, do you want – ?
>No, but I could – .

JAKE.
>Hold onto it. No, maybe you'd better – No, hold onto it. You can always burn it later.
>Fine.

SCILLA.
>What is this?

JAKE.
>No, it's just . . . I'm in a spot of bother with the authorities / but it's no problem, I'm
>sorting it

SCILLA.
>What have you done?

JAKE.
>out, it's more what the sorting out might lead to / because once I start –

SCILLA.
>Are you going to prison?

JAKE.
>No, I'm not going to be in trouble at all by the look of it but that's the problem, I'm
>going to be very – I'm probably paranoid about this.

SCILLA.
>Leave the country. / Are you serious?

JAKE.
>They've taken my passport. I just wanted to let you know in case anything –. I haven't
>mentioned any of this to Dad / but when the shit hits –

SCILLA.
>No, don't get Dad started. Can I do anything?

JAKE.
>No, it's all under control. I feel better talking to you. I didn't go to bed, you know how
>you get in the night. / If anything happens to me –

SCILLA.
>Have some more coffee.
>What? like what?

JAKE.
>Shall I get you another croissant?

SCILLA.
>So what have they found out?

JAKE.
>Jam with it?

SCILLA.
>If you've been making a fortune, I think it's very unfair of you not to have let me in on
>it.

JAKE.
>Forget it.

SCILLA.
So you haven't got Aids. That's great.

SCILLA *and* ZAC *continue.*

SCILLA.
So clearly he was frightened because he'd agreed to tell the DTI who else was involved
(and they'd want to shut him up.)
If I can find out who they are, the murder's halfway solved.
There's plenty of names and numbers here in his diary
So I'll start by contacting anyone who looks interesting and making my own inquiry.

ZAC.
Are you OK?

SCILLA.
Yes, I feel terrific.

ZAC.
You'll just find out a whole lot of colleagues numbers, that won't tell you anything
specific.
My number's probably there for God's sake.

SCILLA.
I'm going to find out who killed Jake.

ZACKERMAN.
Take a sedative, have a sleep, and then see how you feel.

SCILLA.
Nobody sleeps in the middle of a deal.

ZAC.
You've always been lucky, Scilla, don't abuse it.
(I mean, these guys, whoever they are, they could be dangerous.)
You're crazy at the moment, / you're in shock.

SCILLA.
                                    / I'm in shock, I might as well use it.
(I'll let you know what happens.)

ZAC.
Jake's death was a shock for me too, and I kept thinking about a friend of his I'd just
met.
She was called Jacinta Condor and we'd all been doing business together and I knew
she's be quite upset.

ZAC *phones.*

ZAC.
I want to order a number of tropical birds . . . Maybe 20? . . .
Don't tell me what kinds because I won't have heard . . .
Yeah, parrots, cockatoos, marmosets (no, is that a monkey?) lovebirds, sure, stick in
some lovebirds, an assortment in good bright colours, I don't care the exact
number but plenty . . .
No not a cage so much as a small aviary . . .
Deliver it gift wrapped to Jacinta Condor, at the Savoy and the card should read, 'From
Zac, as a small tribute to your beauty and bravery.'

SCILLA *and* GREVILLE *at* GREVILLE'*s house.*

SCILLA.
> Pull yourself together, Daddy.
> What does it matter if Jake was a baddy?

GREVILLE.
> Poor boy. Who would have thought? I'd rather he'd been a failure.
> He used to want to emigrate and sheepfarm in Australia.
> He always would rush in. He had no sense of balance.
> He could have done anything, you know, he had so many talents.
> Musician. Politician. No obstacles in his way.
> If he'd done something else, he'd be alive today.

SCILLA.
> What was he up to, Daddy?
> If it was just insider dealing,
> It's not a proper crime like stealing.
> They say it's a crime without a victim.
> He'd hardly kill himself just because the DTI nicked him.

GREVILLE.
> Dammit, why should he die for something that's not a crime?
> > (It's not illegal in America, Switzerland, Japan, it's only been illegal here the last
> > few years)
> You have to use what you know. You do it all the time.
> That used to be the way you made a reputation.
> By having first class contacts, and first class information.
> One or two greedy people attracted attention to it.
> Suddenly we all pretend Englishmen don't do it.

SCILLA.
> So what was he up to, Daddy?

GREVILLE.
> > I've simply no idea.

SCILLA.
> Do you know who these people are? I've got Jake's diary here.
> Marylou Baines.

GREVILLE.
> Marylou Baines
> Was originally a poor girl from the plains.
> She set out to make whatever she wanted hers
> And now she's one of America's top arbitrageurs.
> > (second only to Boesky)

SCILLA.
> Condor, Jacinta.

GREVILLE.
> A very smart lady from South America who comes here every winter.
> Europe sends aid, her family says thanks
> And buys Eurobonds in Swiss banks.

SCILLA.
> Corman.

GREVILLE.
Billy Corman,
William the Conqueror, the great invader,
A very highly-successful dawn raider.
I don't want to hear any more. Did Jake have friends like this?
I wish he was still a baby and giving daddy a kiss.

SCILLA.
Pull yourself together, daddy.
Did he give you information?

GREVILLE.
                              Absolutely not.

SCILLA.
I thought you might be in on it.

GREVILLE.
                              In on what?

SCILLA.
Then aren't you annoyed he kept it secret from you and didn't share what he'd got?

GREVILLE.
Scilla –

SCILLA.
Jake had powerful friends, that's clear from what you said.
And that means powerful enemies who'd like to see him dead. /
    (He wasn't brave enough to kill himself.)

GREVILLE.
Absolute nonsense.

SCILLA.
I'll start by calling on Corman.

GREVILLE.
                              Security's terribly tight /
He'll never agree to see you.

SCILLA.
Don't worry. I'll get in somehow and see if it gives him a fright.

GREVILLE.
Scilla, you don't seem to realise. Newspapers across the nation.
I could easily lose my job if I lose my reputation.
You and the yobs you work with are hardly worth a mention,
    (no one expects them to have any standards)
But I have to keep very quiet, and not attract attention.
Until it's all blown over I think I'll stay in bed.

SCILLA.
You never liked me, Daddy. Jake was always your favourite.

GREVILLE.
I don't like the louts you work with.

SCILLA.
                              And now you've got to pay for it.

GREVILLE.
Poor Scilla, are you suffering from feelings of rejection?

SCILLA.
If I find out you were in on it, you're not getting my protection.

GREVILLE.
    (In on killing Jakey?)

SCILLA.
    (In on anything.)

GREVILLE.
Darling, don't be difficult when I'm so awfully sad. /
I think Jakey was playing in a bigger league than Dad.

SCILLA.
I've always been ashamed of you. Your drink and your pomposity.

GREVILLE.
Scilla, the oiks you work with have made you a monstrosity.

SCILLA.
If I find you're implicated in my investigation / the News of the World can have you.

GREVILLE.
Darling, you always did have a vivid imagination
    (like poor Mummy.)

ZAC.
When I left Scilla I rushed back to work because Corman's bid for Albion was just
    reaching its peak.
He'd been spending the night in the office the whole of that week.
We'd been building to this since the day a few months ago
When Albion started, just one of several deals, easy and slow.
It started like this:

CORMAN *a corporate raider.* BROWN *and* SMITH, *industrial spies.* ZAC.
MRS ETHERINGTON, *a stockbroker.*

CORMAN.
The analysts reports are satisfactory,
Predicting high industrial synergy.
I'll have to close the chocolate biscuit factory.
The management lacks drive and energy.
Tell me what you learnt about the company.

BROWN.
I spent a month posing as a secretary.
The working atmosphere is very pleasant.
A shock to the chairman would be salutary,
His presence at his desk is just symbolic,
He disappears to fish and shoot pheasant.
The managing director's alcoholic,
But still he's everybody favourite,
His drink 'n' driving ends him up in court,

He gets the company to pay for it.
The middle management are sound but lazy,
The details will be found in my report.
The chief of marketing is going crazy.

CORMAN.
Excellent, they'll put up no resistance.
I'll sack them all, put in new staff, maybe promote a few of their assistants.
Too late for them to make the company over,
Because I am going to take the company over.
Now to the larger and still more inviting
Albion Products. Fuck the analysts,
What do they know? It's that much more exciting.
Is their chairman gaga too and their managing director always pissed?

SMITH.
No, he's sober and quite competent.
Duckett runs a rather happy ship.
I hear the head of sales is impotent,
A very old director broke his hip,
Apart from that they all seem quite efficient.
Employees feel considerable loyalty.
The factory has been visited by royalty.

CORMAN.
Albion is obviously deficient
In management. Old-fashioned and paternal.
These figures stink. I can make it earn a l-
ot more for its shareholders, who are
The owners after all. It will be far
Better run, streamlined, rationalised,
When it forms part of Corman Enterprise.
    (And anyway I want it.)
Right. Both targets will be hit.
Now summon my war cabinet.

CORMAN.
Zac, I really like this company.

ZAC.
It'll take some stalking. It's a big confident beast.

CORMAN.
But I'm told you're a takeover artiste.
Can you get it for me?

ZAC.
Corman, you're the buyer./
I pride myself I can acquire any company the client

CORMAN.
Anyway, if it was easy it'd bore me.

ZAC.
may desire.
    (If I was defending Albion you wouldn't stand a chance.)
We're going to need a whole lot of finance from somewhere.

CORMAN.
Zackerman, that's your ride on the funfair.

Now Etherington. I want you to start a stealthy
Purchase of Albion stock. Don't frighten them.
The price must hardly move, just look quite healthy.
We'll put nooses round their necks and suddenly tighten them.

ETHERINGTON.
Albion's price is 310.
I shall acquire twenty million ordinary
Shares on your behalf, imperceptibly.
And I shall let you know of any change.

ZAC.
We've got to get out here and ride the range.

ETHERINGTON.
I don't think you'll find me lacking in assiduity.

CORMAN.
I'm a great admirer of Etherington's ingenuity.
    (Top brokers for fuck's sake, what do you think I am? Brokers to royalty.)
When we tell Duckett I own five per cent
    (plus what else I'll control by then)
He'll suddenly wonder where his company went.

DUCKETT.

DUCKETT.
I'm Duckett. I enjoy the *Financial Times*.
It's fun reading about other people's crimes.
My company Albion's price is looking perky.
I think I'll buy that villa in the south of Turkey.

CORMAN, ETHERINGTON, ZAC.

CORMAN.
So what's on the agenda today?
Let's get all the rubbish out of the way.

ETHERINGTON
We're failing to acquire Mayfield.

CORMAN.
                          Except I never fail.
Why don't I suggest we'll leave them alone, provided they pay us greenmail?
    (American term, greenbacks, blackmail, everybody happy?)

ZAC.
If they really want to defend themselves they'll do a leveraged management buyout to
    get back their shares.

ETHERINGTON.
So we make a hundred million.

CORMAN.
And the lousy company's still theirs.

ZAC.
(Plus a whole lot of debt.
In the US there's an oil company borrowed four billion dollars to fight off T.Boone
Pickens and now they're paying three million a day interest.)

CORMAN.
So that money goes to improving our position
With Albion, my favourite acquisition.
How we doing?

ETHERINGTON.
The Albion share is up to 315
And you now own 4.9% /
Not 5%, so no need to disclose.

CORMAN.
Excellent.
So now?

ETHERINGTON.
Now we contact institutions,
The pension fund managers who hold
Millions of Corman shares and indicate
It would be wise to lend us their support.

ZAC.
Can we rely on them?

ETHERINGTON.
They won't say no,
For otherwise a succulent new issue
Next time we have one might not come their way.

CORMAN.
It's their duty to keep our price up after all.
The poor old pensioners won't want it to fall.

ETHERINGTON.
We also intimate it's in their interest
To buy up Albion so that more and more
Albion shares belong to friends of ours. /
A fan club and not a concert party.

ZAC.
A concert party.

CORMAN.
Come on, don't fart
About, it's a concert party.

ETHERINGTON.
A fan club (of disinterested supporters) is respectable and legal.

A concert party (of people you've induced to support you) reprehensible.
This is a line you may trust us to tread /
(as long as necessary)

CORMAN.
Tread in the shit. Tread where you need to tread.
Now purchases must also be-made by Metgee, Upkate,
Battershot, Mountainring

ZAC.
and Stoneark.

CORMAN.
Five nominee companies registered in the Turks and Caicos Islands, Panama and Sark.
They can each acquire 4.9%.

ZACKERMAN.
And one of our problems is solved.
You'll acquire a huge share in Albion without anyone suspecting you're involved.

ETHERINGTON.
We're still left with a cashflow problem.
Albion's more than three times as big as Corman.

CORMAN.
Zac, you understand how a buyer works.
Time you stepped in and showed us a few fireworks.

ZAC.
The last couple of years in the United States it's been takeover mania
And I guess the deals there have gotten somewhat zanier.
Junk bonds are a quick way of raising cash, but it's kind of a hit 'n'
    run method, which doesn't go down too well in Britain.
You don't have millions of private investors crazy to gamble on debt.

ETHERINGTON.
No, you wouldn't succeed with junk bonds here just yet.
But the British public's financial education
Is going in leaps and bounds with privatisation.
Sid will buy junk soon. / Just wait.

ZAC.
Great.

CORMAN.
So no junk. How do we stand with the loan?
Can you show us some tricks?

ZAC.
The money can be supplied from a number of banks here and in the United States led
    by our own.
I got the rate of interest down a couple of ticks.
In return they want us to mortgage Upkate, Battershot and Stoneark, and form five
    new nominee companies so we can wind up Albion and redistribute its assets,
Which gives us tax neutral benefits.
We repay the loan and the interest by selling off certain sections of Albion after it's
    been acquired.

CORMAN.
Some people might think I'm a touch overgeared.
Our ratio of debt to equity is –?

ETHERINGTON.

Four hundred per cent.

CORMAN.
Taking into account the billion and a half you've lent.
(But being in debt is the best way to be rich.)

ZAC.
(America's national debt is over a trillion dollars.)

CORMAN.
So we've got the money. [*to* ETHERINGTON.] Get out there and spend it.
We've got Albion.

ZAC.
No, let's wait and see how Duckett's going to defend it.
(Poison pills? shark repellent?)

ETHERINGTON.
If Albion's shares should fall some of our friends would be in for a shock.

ZAC.
A deposit with us could provide a guarantee.

CORMAN.
And then there's the question of buying Corman stock.
To buy your own shares is illegal and cannot be.

ZAC.
But the bank can buy them, no problem and we'll let you know later about our fee.

CORMAN.
Zackerman, my very sincere thanks.
This is the kind of service I expect from our banks.
Etherington, I'm sure you've plenty to do.
I'll join you later for a glass of poo.

ETHERINGTON *goes.*

We don't breathe a word of this to anyone.
But someone could breathe a word to Marylou.
I think she could step in here and have some fun.
But I don't want direct contact and nor should you.

ZAC.
No problem.

CORMAN *goes.*

So I called Jake Todd.

ZAC *and* JAKE *drinking in champagne bar. Late night. Both drunk.*

JAKE.
What did you think of the family?

ZAC.
Quite a mansion.

JAKE.
>You could buy yourself something equally handsome.
>(Or three.)

ZAC.
>Why do the British always want land?
>(In Paris or New York you live in an apartment, why do the English need gardens?)

JAKE.
>You're not upper class without it, you're too American to understand.

ZAC.
>You don't make money out of land, you make money out of money.

JAKE.
>It's a dream. Woods. Springtime. Owning the spring.
>What's so funny?

ZAC.
>Is that your dream?

JAKE.
>   I never dream. / (I never sleep)

ZAC.
>   Because it's come to an end.
>Young kids like you making money now – and I mean the ones who've never had it, not like you – they're going to come up with new ways to spend
>Because they're going to come up with new dreams.

JAKE.
>I'll tell you, Zac, sometimes it seems . . .

ZAC.
>What?

JAKE.
>I don't know, what were we saying?

ZAC.
>When?

JAKE.
>Forget it. /
>Tell you something. I fancy the ocean.
>Instead of land. I'd like to own a big cube of sea, right down to the bottom, all the fish, weeds, the lot.
>There'd be takers for that.

ZAC.
>   Sure, it's a great notion.

JAKE.
>Or air. Space. A square metre going straight up into infinity.

ZAC.
>And a section of God at the top.

JAKE.

Oh yes, I'll make you a market in divinity (any day.)

MARYLOU BAINES *and* TK *in New York*

TK.

There's a message from Jake Todd in London.
He recommends buying shares in Albion.

MARYLOU.

Can I take it this is so far completely secret?

TK.

Yes, when it gets out it'll really move the market.

MARYLOU.

Are you trading in this stock on your own account?

TK.

Not for a very considerable amount.

MARYLOU.

You'll soon be setting up your own show.

TK.

No, Ms Baines, I wouldn't go, you taught me everything I know.
I really admire your style, Miss Baines.
    (You're a great American.)

MARYLOU.

Sure, arbitrage is a service to the community,
And it's too bad they're prosecuting people you'd have thought would have had
    immunity.
By buying and selling large amounts of stock we ensure the market's liquidity –
I work twenty-hour days and take pills for stomach acidity –
So companies can be taken over easy,
Which means discharging superfluous workers, discontinuing unprofitable
    lines, the kind of stuff that makes your lazy inefficient management queasy.
So considering the good we do the US economy,
I reckon we should be treated with a little more respect and bonhomie.

I have a hundred and fifty telephone lines because I depend on information.

TK.

    (What's the least a person could start with?

MARYLOU.

    I started small – say twenty?)
You need to know what's going on in businesses all over the nation,

TK.

    (And Britain)

MARYLOU.

You take a lot of gambles, / which keeps the adrenalin flowing and is why it's known as
    risk arbitrage,

TK.
(Ms Baines, I admire your guts)

MARYLOU.
Though if you know how to get the right information the risk isn't all that large.

TK.
But since Boesky was caught out –

MARYLOU.
Sure, some of our informants are more cautious,
But information's what it's all about,
So I reckon it's business as usual and only now and then does nervousness make me
    nauseous.
You and I both know what it's like to have other guys stepping on your head,
And you can't get on when you're dead.

TK.
So you think it's worth me giving it a shot?

MARYLOU.
Get out, TK, and give it all you've got.
After all, what happens if you fail?

TK.
I end up broke and in jail.

MARYLOU.
Look, with his own collapse Boesky did the biggest insider deal of all:
The SEC let him unload over a billion dollars worth of shares ahead of announcing his
    fall.
So paying a hundred million dollar fine was pretty minimal.
Which is great, because he overstepped some regulations, sure, but the guy's no
    criminal.
Like he said about his own amazing wealth.
'Greed is all right. Greed is healthy. You can be greedy and still feel good about
    yourself.'

Buy twenty million shares in Albion today.
(That's in addition to what you've bought.)
In a few weeks when Corman announces the bid and the price shoots up, we sell quick,
    take the profit, and on our way.

DUCKETT, *chairman of* ALBION, *and* MS BIDDULPH, *a white knight. Both from the
    north.*

DUCKETT.
Biddulph, I'm desperate. Corman's going to take over Albion. Shall I pay him
greenmail and take on half a billion debt? Shall I do one of those American things,
poison pills, shark repellant, make some arrangement so the company comes to bits
if he gets hold of it? Shall I cash in my Eurobond and emigrate?

BIDDULPH.
Now Duckett, you're under quite serious attack.
It's time to fight back.

DUCKETT.

I'd like to fight back.

BIDDULPH.

I know you'd give Corman a terrible fright
If you had a white knight.

DUCKETT.

I'd like a white knight.

BIDDULPH.

Now Corman will throw the top management out
But I'd guarantee that your job would remain.

DUCKETT.
Say it again?

BIDDULPH.

Your job would remain.
But Corman would throw the top management out.
That's what it's about.

DUCKETT.

That's what it's about.
But you'd guarantee that my job would remain.

BIDDULPH.
So if I should step in would I have your support?

DUCKETT.
Would you have my support!

BIDDULPH.

That's just what I thought.

DUCKETT.
It's very unfair to be attacked like this. I run a highly efficient company. I've sacked the finance director and the chief of marketing who'd both been with the company ten years. I've closed two factories and made five hundred people redundant. No one can say I'm not a hardhitting management.

BIDDULPH.
Hold on, Duckett, you've got it all wrong. Think of it from the PR angle. You're an old-fashioned firm. A good old English firm that has the loyalty of its employees and the support of the local community. You spend a lot of money on research and development.

DUCKETT.
I spend some, I suppose, but I always consider the shareholders' dividend and the short-term –

BIDDULPH.
No no no, you consider the long term. You're the kind of company the CBI likes. Corman means short-term profit. You mean industrial development. Think of Pilkington, Duckett. You're loved locally. Children like you. Dogs.

DUCKETT.
What I dream of you know is cornering the coffee market. Brazil needs to be hammered into the ground and the price kept right down low and –

BIDDULPH.
No, Duckett, not at the moment.

You're a sweet English maiden, all shining and bright.
And Corman's the villain intent upon rape
And I'm the white knight

DUCKETT.
You're the white knight

BIDDULPH.
And the knight has a fight and the maiden escapes
And when I'm in charge I'll put everything right.
(We can talk about closing Scunthorpe later.)

ZAC.

ZAC.
Jake couldn't have picked a worse time to die if he hated my guts.
Corman hadn't slept for forty-eight hours and was driving himself and everyone else
nuts.
Jake was my one real friend over here. It's not that I don't care,
But the deal could get clinched today and I just don't have the attention to spare.
(If he's put me in the shit with the DTI I'll worry about that later.)

CORMAN, ZAC, ETHERINGTON and others of CORMAN'S team.

CORMAN.
Right, you all know the position,
Biddulph's stepped in as a white knight to stop us making the acquisition.
Don't worry, she hasn't a chance, it's just a try on.
We've 15% of Albion stock plus 20% fan club holdings whose votes we can rely on.
Two aims:
One. Boost our own share price by getting anyone at all to buy Corman stock to
increase the value of our offer. Two. Get anyone at all who'll vote for us to buy up
Albion shares.
So in a word, get anyone you can by any means you can to buy both our stock and
theirs.
From today we're coming to the crunch.
Nobody's going out any more to lunch.
(You can cancel dinner too.)
From today, we're going for the gold.
Put your family life and your sex life on hold.
A deal like this, at the start you gently woo it.
There comes a time when you get in there and screw it.
So you get the stock. And I don't care how you do it.

ETHERINGTON.
My reputation for integrity
Compels me to suggest you should take care.
No point succeeding if that same success
Destroys you and your company forever.
Remember Guinness.

CORMAN.
>   Thank you, Etherington. Some of us have work to do here.

ZAC.
>   There's no question there are thin lines and this is definitely a grey area.
>   And since Guinness it's a whole lot scarier.
>   You can't play ball if you keep off the grass.
>   So promise whatever you have to. Peddle your ass.
>   Let's give it all we've got and worry later.

CORMAN (*to* ETHERINGTON).
>   Are you standing there as some kind of arbitrator?
>   You can piss off, I'll get another broker.
>   The last thing I need in my pack is some tight-arsed joker.
>> (I thought you were good at this.)

ETHERINGTON.
>   My duty has been done in speaking out.
>   And now I'll help in every way I can.
>   My reputation for integrity
>   Will reassure our colleagues of their safety
>   In making any purchase we advise.

CORMAN.
>   Then let's get on / with it.

ZAC.
>   Let's get on with it, guys.

OTHERS *on phones.*

This works as a round i.e., each starts at slash in previous speech and continues with all speeches as long as required. At end of each speech, each shouts out the amount of stock the person at the other end of the phone has agreed to buy e.g., twenty thousand, a hundred thousand.

1. If you were interested in acquiring some Corman stock/ there is a considerable sum on deposit with Klein Merrick so / in the event of any subsequent fall in the share price you would be guaranteed against loss – 20,000

2. If you were interested in buying some Albion stock / there would be no question of being unable to dispose of them at a price at least equal to what you gave – 100,000

3. If you were able to see your way to supporting the bid / the new Albion under Corman management would naturally look favourably at any tenders for office cleaning that compared favourably with our present arrangements –

4. If you should be interested in following our recommendation to acquire Corman stock, an interest free loan could be arranged at once with which the purchase could be made –

>   *Meanwhile:*

ZAC (*on phone*).
>   Remember me to Vanessa and the boys.
>   Listen, Corman, this may just be a rumour,
>   But if it's true it doesn't appeal to my sense of humour.
>   I've just had a word with a colleague in Atlanta & Gulf.
>   Marylou's been dealing with Biddulph.
>   I think it's time you spoke to her yourself.

CORMAN.
>Dealing with Biddulph? I just sent her some flowers.
>What the fuck does she think – ? She's meant to be one of ours.
>I tried to call her this morning but I got the machine.
>Leave a message after the tone? I'll leave something obscene.

CORMAN phones MARYLOU.

CORMAN.
>Marylou? You got the flowers? A tragic bereavement.

MARYLOU.
>Yes, TK made a real pretty arrangement.

CORMAN.
>And our pretty arrangement's still OK?

MARYLOU.
>I did dispose of a large holding today.

CORMAN.
>You what? Disposed? A large Albion holding?
>I gave you that on the clear understanding –

MARYLOU.
>No, Corman, don't pursue it.
>Anything I do I just happen to do because I want to do it.

CORMAN.
>You owe me, Marylou.

MARYLOU.
>I owe you?
>I'm not even certain that I know you.

Unnoticed by CORMAN *or* ZAC, SCILLA *arrives, explaining herself quietly to one of* CORMAN's *team.*

SCILLA.
>Kissogram for Mr Corman from Marylou Baines.

Meanwhile CORMAN *and* MARYLOU *continue:*

CORMAN.
>How much Albion did you have?

MARYLOU.
>15%.

CORMAN.
>Can I just ask you where the hell it went?

MARYLOU.
>Don't be slow, Bill. That's quite upsetting
>I like to think I'm dealing with an equal.

CORMAN.
>Marylou, it's not that I'm not smart.
>It's just hard to believe you'd break my heart.
>Biddulph? Biddulph? what? you knew you were getting
>Information from me / via Zackerman via Jake Todd.

MARYLOU.
You can't predict the sequel.

CORMAN.
But you knew Jake Todd was one of mine.

MARYLOU.
You are slow, / Bill.

CORMAN.
Because he's dead? you didn't want to be connected
With Jake now he's dead in case someone suspected – /
So that's why you sold to Biddulph.

MARYLOU.
I hope these phones are adequately scrambled.

CORMAN.
I don't give a fuck who else is on the line.
You cheated me. / I hate you. I'll fucking annihilate you.

MARYLOU.
Corman, you'll get rumbled
If you don't keep your temper. Be glad you're alive,
(as my very irritating old aunty used to say.)
Don't worry about it. What's 15%? Get after the other 85.

MARYLOU *hangs up.*

ZAC.
We need her.

CORMAN *calls* MARYLOU *back.*

CORMAN.
Marylou? You know how it is. You say things in haste.
Our friendship's far too important / to waste

MARYLOU.
What do you want, Bill?

CORMAN.
Can you see your way to going back into Albion?
Will you buy Corman and support our price?
Smashing Biddulph would be very nice /
If you've anything –

MARYLOU.
Bill I'd be glad to do something for you / but

CORMAN.
I understand your problem, how can I reassure you?

MARYLOU.
I'm playing with about a billion
But most of that's occupied over here.
If I had another hundred million
In my investment fund,
Then I guess / I'd have a freer hand.

CORMAN.
I think I can probably see my way clear.
This is hardly the moment with so much else on our minds.
But I had been meaning for some time to approach you with a view to becoming a
   contributor to your investment fund because I have of course the greatest
   admiration/ for your wide experience and market timing

MARYLOU.
I could have my people send you some documentation.

   MARYLOU *hangs up.*
   SCILLA *approaches* CORMAN *and sings.*

SCILLA.
Happy takeover day.
Take Albion away.
Happy takeover, Corman.
Happy takeover day.

CORMAN.
What the hell?

SCILLA.
Kissogram from Marylou Baines.

CORMAN.
From Marylou Baines? I'll kill her.

SCILLA.
I'm not really. I'm Jake Todd's sister, Scilla.

ZAC.
What the –

CORMAN.
What?

SCILLA.
    Jake Todd's sister.

CORMAN.
Is this a terrorist a-/
ttack?

SCILLA.
I heard you. 'Jake Todd was one of mine.'
Tell me what it's all about. /
Did someone kill Jake?

CORMAN.
Will someone please get this lunatic out?

ZAC.
Hold it, hold it, everything's fine.
I know her, it's OK, she's not insane, she won't be armed, don't press
The security button, we'll be held up for hours with water sprinklers and the SAS. /
   (Let's get on with the job here.)

SCILLA.
You killed my brother.

CORMAN.
    Zac.

ZAC.
    He didn't / he really didn't. I'm certain he didn't.

CORMAN.
    Do you work for Marylou Baines?
        (Because you can tell her from me –)

SCILLA.
    No, that was a trick to get in. / Now will you explain

CORMAN.
    (Don't work for her.)

SCILLA.
    What 'one of mine' means. One of your what?
    He did something illegal. You were frightened of what he'd say
    To the DTI and you wanted him out of the way.
    Tell me what's going on or I'll tell the press
    My brother was acting for you the night he was shot.
    Did you kill him yourself or get your broker to pull the trigger?

CORMAN.
    After the deal, after the deal I'll confess
    To murdering anyone just let me get on with the deal.

SCILLA.
    You and Zac got Jake into some mess.
    He did little fiddles but this must have been much bigger.
    You and Zac got him involved in some corrupt / ring

CORMAN.
    Suppose I had killed Jake, his ghost would have had more sense than walk in here today
        and interrupt. /

ZAC.
    Can you spare me for five minutes?

CORMAN.
    He got on because he knew what was a priority / and he'd have reckoned

SCILLA.
    He got on. Doing what exactly?

CORMAN.
    That matters of life and death came a poor second.

ZAC.
    Can you spare me for five minutes?

CORMAN.
    No, not for two. / Go on.

SCILLA.
    I'm not leaving here / until you

ZAC.
    I'll tell you. / I'll tell you.

SCILLA.
You will.

CORMAN.
You'll what?

ZAC.
Can I handle this? Can I just handle this please?

ZAC *and* SCILLA *outside* CORMAN*'s office.*

SCILLA.
So tell me.

ZAC.
Marylou Baines – we'll make it quick, OK? /
Needs inside information and she's willing to pay.

SCILLA.
You knew all this this morning and you didn't say.

ZAC.
So anyone in London with news would give it to Jake,
And he'd get half a percent / on whatever she'd make.

SCILLA.
Half a percent?
That meant . . .

ZAC.
If she made fifty million –

SCILLA.
                    He got two hundred and fifty thousand.
If she made two hundred million / – he never told me.

ZAC.
I think little Jakey could have bought and sold me.
So now you know, OK? And now you drop it.

SCILLA.
What do you mean? / I'm just getting started.

ZAC.
I've got work to do.

SCILLA.
Who killed him? Corman? You?

ZAC.
                    I'm too tenderhearted
And Corman's too busy. Scilla, stop it.
We have to keep this quiet now. Face the facts.
You're never going to find out all Jake's contacts.
Let it go. I've got work to do. Don't get in a state.

SCILLA.
You knew all along. He never told me. Wait.

ZAC *goes.*

He was making serious money.

SCILLA.
> So Zac went back to Corman and I thought I'd better go to work despite Jake being
> dead because Chicago comes in at one twenty and I hate to miss it. I work on the floor
> of LIFFE, the London International Financial Futures Exchange.

> Trading options and futures looks tricky if you don't understand it.
> But if you're good at market timing you can make out like a bandit.
>> (It's the most fun I've had since playing cops and robbers with Jake when we were
>> children.)
> A simple way of looking at futures is take a commodity,
> Coffee, cocoa, sugar, zinc, pork bellies, copper, aluminium, oil –
>> I always think pork bellies is an oddity.
>> (They could just as well have a future in chicken wings.)
> Suppose you're a coffee trader and there's a drought in Brazil like last year or suppose
>> there's a good harvest, either way you might lose out,
> So you can buy a futures contract that works in the opposite direction so you're covered
>> against loss, and that's what futures are basically about.
> But of course you don't have to take delivery of anything at all.
> You can buy and sell futures contracts without any danger of ending up with ten tons of
>> pork bellies in the hall.

> On the floor of LIFFE the commodity is money.
> You can buy and sell money, you can buy and sell absence of money, debt, which used
>> to strike me as funny.

> For some it's hedging, for most it's speculation.
> In New York they've just introduced a futures contract in inflation.
>> (Pity it's not Bolivian inflation, which hit forty thousand per cent.)

> I was terrified when I started because there aren't many girls and they line up to watch
>> you walk,
> And every time I opened my mouth I felt self-conscious because of the way I talk.
> I found O levels weren't much use, the best qualified people are street traders.
> But I love it because it's like playing a cross between roulette and space invaders.

LIFFE canteen.

SCILLA. JOANNE *a runner.* KATHY *a trader.*

JOANNE.
> I said I'm not going to work down there.
> It's like animals in a zoo. / So then I thought I'll have a bash.

KATHY.
> When you start they really stare.

SCILLA.
> Don't let them see you care.

JOANNE.
> I'll never learn what to do. / I'll never learn hand signals.

SCILLA.
> I couldn't walk across the floor / my first day.

KATHY.
> This morning's really a bore, / there's nothing happening.

JOANNE.
  I answered a telephone / for the first time.

KATHY.
  You really feel on your own.

SCILLA.
  Never say hold on / because they don't hold on.

KATHY.
  I can manage two phones at once but not three.

SCILLA.
  Sometimes I've put the phone down because I don't know what they're saying.

JOANNE.
  You do get used to the noise, I nearly fainted the first day.

KATHY.
  I can deal without shouting, most of them like shouting.

SCILLA.
  Men are just little boys. / Dave had lost twenty slips at the end of yesterday and
    muggins finds them for him.

JOANNE.
  Terry asked me out this morning. He was the first person who spoke to me on my first
    day, he was really friendly.
  Is it all right going out? / Do they talk about you?

SCILLA.
  You do get talked about, / I hear so and so's knocking off so and so.

KATHY.
  Just go out for lunch, / then nothing can happen after.

SCILLA.
  They're a very chauvinist bunch.

KATHY.
  We've all been out with Terry.

SCILLA.
  Anyway they're all too knackered / by the end of the day.

KATHY.
  It's true, they're all frustrated / because they never have time to do it.

JOANNE.
  I'm completely exhausted.
  At midnight I'm washing my knickers / because I'm too speedy to sleep.

KATHY.
  I get up at half-past five and have a good breakfast.

SCILLA.
  Mind you, I like Terry.

  TERRY, DAVE, MARTIN, BRIAN *and* VINCE, traders, arrive.

KATHY.
  Hello, Terry.

TERRY.
    What about Saturday?

JOANNE.
    I don't know.

TERRY.
    Think about it.

KATHY.
    Better be getting back.

MARTIN.
    Time we did some work. Nearly time for Chicago.

VINCE.
    Coming out with me tonight?

SCILLA.
    Leave it out, Vince.

DAVE.
    Leave the lady alone.

VINCE (*to* JOANNE).
    Coming out with me tonight?

KATHY.
    Leave it out, Vince.

Floor of LIFFE. Four separate companies each with their phones, and a trading pit.
Klein Merrick has SCILLA *on the phone,* TERRY *and* DAVE *on the floor,* MANDY *as runner.*
2 – has SHERILL *on the phone,* MARTIN *and* KATHY *on the floor,* PETE *as runner.*
3 – has DICK *on the phone,* BRIAN *and* JILL *on the floor,* JOANNE *as runner.*
4 – has MARY *on the phone,* VINCE *and* JOHN *on the floor,* ANNIE *as runner.*
They all start going to their places. As ANNIE, *who is new, walks down the lads cheer and jeer.*

TERRY.
    You're in late.

SCILLA.
    Trouble at home. My brother's been shot.

TERRY.
    You what?

SCILLA.
    There's going to be a scandal.

TERRY.
    Another one? / Did you say your brother?

SCILLA.
    Bigger.

TERRY.
    Is it worth trading on?

SCILLA.
There might be a run on sterling if you're lucky.

KATHY.
Ere come the c'nardlies.

BRIAN.
Fuck off, sweaty git.

DICK.
Fuck off, dogbreath.

BRIAN.
Yeh, lovely. I'll feel better when I get rid of these oysters.

SCILLA.
Dave! Dave!

BRIAN.
And how are you this morning?

JILL.
Don't talk to me, I'm all fucked up.

JOANNE.
Do you call him Dick because he's got spots?

JILL.
No, I call him Spot because he's a dick.

VINCE.
Annie, if you sell the front and buy the back, / you'll be short of front and long of back.

BRIAN.
Muff city, no pity.

SCILLA.
Dave, Grimes says Zac's got a ten million rollover for March so sell 10 at 9. If you can't get it he'll go to 8. And 15 June at your best price.

TERRY.
Are you Annie? Can you find this guy and give him a message.

ANNIE.
Mike who?

TERRY.
Hunt.

KATHY.
I'm tired of making money for other people. I'd like to be a local.

SCILLA.
Oi! Dave! You can't signal with a pencil in your hand.

DAVE.
Just fuckin have, haven't I.

KATHY.
The theoretical spread is too large.[1]

JOANNE.
Did you see that actor from the Bill who was in here yesterday?

KATHY.
  I saw him first.

JOANNE.
  I saw him first.

KATHY.
  I wonder if he'll come back.

JOANNE.
  I wonder if he's married.

  Trading is now getting going.

JOANNE.
  What do you want this morning?

PETE.
  She wants 18 at 15.

JOANNE.
  All I want is a bacon roll.

PETE (*sings*).
  All I want is a bacon roll.

  Meanwhile:

DAVE.
  [1]Red June is showing 4 bid for 5.

TERRY.
  Sterling showing 5 at 3.

DICK (*phone*).
  March showing 9.
  (*To* BRIAN *on floor.*) 5 at 9. 5 at 9.
  (*Another phone call.*) Is that another 5 or the same 5?
  (*To* BRIAN.) 5 more at 9. 5 more. 10 at 9. 10 at 9.

BRIAN.
  5 at 9 filled.[2]

DICK (*phone*).
  Your first 5 at 9 filled.

SHERILL.
  We want 20 out of Footsie and into gilts.[3]
  (*To* MARTIN.) Sell 20 at 1. 20 at 1.
  (*To* KATHY.) Bid 9 for 20, 9 for 20.

MARTIN.
  20 at 1.

KATHY.
  9 for 20.

MARY.
  [2]March gilts 8 rising fast. Do you want to sell now or wait? They might go another two
  ticks if you're lucky. (*To floor.*) 5 at 9. 5 at 9.

BRIAN.
  [3]Where we going tonight?

TERRY.
The old Chinese?

BRIAN.
Dragon city, no pity.

DAVE.
I'll tell Vince.

BRIAN.
Oi, we're 18 for 15.

TERRY.
18 for 15. Working 20.

DAVE.
Table for 15 please.

JOHN.
10 at 19. 10 at 19.

VINCE.
John John John – just 5 at 19.
You can't trust John's bids.

MARY.
He's had too many beers.

DAVE.
I've got a certain winner for the 3.30 if anyone's interested.[4]

BRIAN.
You haven't paid us yesterday's winnings yet.

DAVE.
Leave it out, Brian, I always pay you.

KATHY.
[4]Come on gilts. 2 at 4 the gilts.

MARTIN.
Sterling showing 5 at 3.

TERRY.
Euro 4 bid now.

SCILLA.
Dave, you're supposed to be looking at me right?

DAVE.
Am I in or am I out?[5]

MANDY.
You gotta listen. If you don't listen we can't get in touch with you.

DAVE.
What?

SCILLA.
If you look at me I won't give you stick.

VINCE.
[5]10 bid for 70. Let's get some stock away.

MARTIN.
  Whare the fuck have you been?

PETE.
  Oh I see, you're not even allowed to crap.

MARTIN.
  If Tony rings tell him I can't get out.

BRIAN.
  I'm long on Footsie.

DAVE.
  Don't know why I bothered coming in today.

MARTIN.
  It's really flying. / It's really going somewhere.

SCILLA (*to* MANDY).
  Find out if Brian bought 20 off Dave at 6.

MANDY *goes to* BRIAN.

MANDY.
  Did you buy 20 off Dave at 6?[6]

BRIAN.
  Going to the Greenhouse tonight?

DICK (*to* BRIAN).
  [6]5 at 9. Have you got that second 5 at 9 filled?

JILL (*to* BRIAN).
  Have you got that second 5 at 9 filled?

BRIAN.
  Leave me alone, I'm talking to the young lady.[7]

ANNIE *comes up to* BRIAN.

ANNIE.
  I'm looking for Mike Hunt.

BRIAN.
  She's looking for her cunt.

ANNIE *realises and starts to cry.* MANDY *takes her back to her trading booth.*

MANDY.
  Don't worry, they do it to everyone when they're new.

SHERILL.
  OUT OUT OUT!
  [7]John, phone for you.

JOHN *hears on the phone that his and* DAVE's *horse won. He rushes to find* DAVE *and they embrace and jump up and down.*

JOHN.
  Dave, the horse! It won!

DAVE.
  I fucking won two thousand pounds!

Furious trading now starts. Everyone flat out. Among the things we hear:

VINCE.
> 6 for 10. 6 for 10.

JOHN.
> 10 at 6. 10 at 6.

VINCE.
> I'm buying at 6, you cunt.

SHERRILL (*on phone*).
> 11 coming 10, 11 coming 10, 11 10 11 10, 10! 10 10 10 10 coming 9, 10 coming 9, etc.

BRIAN.
> What's your fucking game?

MARTIN.
> Oh fuck off.

BRIAN.
> I'll fucking break your leg, you fucking cunt.

SCILLA (*to* DAVE).
> You'll have to shout louder if you can't signal better.

BRIAN (*to* DAVE).
> You're trading like a cunt.

Out of furious trading emerges the song:

FUTURES SONG

Out you cunt, out in oh fuck it
I've dealt the gelt below the belt and I'm jacking up the ackers
My front's gone short, fuck off old sport, you're standing on my knackers
I've spilt my guts, long gilt's gone nuts and I think I'm going crackers
So full of poo I couldn't screw, I fucked it with my backers
> I fucked it with my backers
> I fucked it with my backers

Backups: Out! Buy buy buy! Leave it!
> No! Yes! Cunt!
> 4! 5! Sell!
> Quick! Prick! Yes! No! Cunt!

How hard I dredge to earn my wedge, I'm sharper than a knife
Don't fucking cry get out and buy, Chicago's going rife
You're back to front come on you cunt don't give me any strife
You in or out? Don't hang about, you're on the floor of Liffe!

They call me a tart who can hardly fart when it's bedlam in the pit
I'm the local tootsie playing footsie but I don't mind a bit
Cos my future trusts my money lusts as far as it can spit
And my sterling works on mouthy jerks whose bids are full of shit

I'm a Romford scholar in eurodollars and June is showing four
Botham out nineteen on the Reuters screen is the very latest score
I fucked that runner she's a right little stunner so I pulled her off the floor
I was bidding straight till my interest rate jumped up and asked for more

Money-making money-making money-making money-making
Money-making money-making money-making caper
Do the fucking business do the fucking business do the fucking business
And bang it down on paper

So L.I.F.F.E. is the life for me and I'll burn out when I'm dead
And this fair exchange is like a rifle range what's the price of flying lead?
When you soil your jeans on soya beans shove some cocoa up your head
You can never hide if your spread's too wide, you'll just fuck yourself instead.

ACT II

JACINTA CONDOR *flying first class.*

JACINTA.
Flight to England that little grey island in the clouds where governments don't fall overnight and children don't sell themselves in the street and my money is safe. I'll buy a raincoat, I'll meet Jake Todd, I'll stay at the Savoy by the stream they call a river with its Bloody Tower and dead queens, a river is too wide to bridge. The unfinished bridge across the canyon where the road ends in the air, waiting for dollars. The office blocks father started, imagining glass, leather, green screens, the city rising high into the sky, but the towers stopped short, cement, wires, the city spreading wider instead with a blur of shacks, miners coming down from the mountains as the mines close. The International Tin Council, what a scandal, thank God I wasn't in tin, the price of copper ruined by the frozen exchange rate, the two rates, and the government will not let us mining companies exchange enough dollars at the better rate, they insist we help the country in this crisis, I do not want to help, I want to be rich, I close my mines and sell my copper on the London Metal Exchange. It is all because of the debt that will never be paid because we have to borrow more and more to pay the interest on the money that came from oil when OPEC had too much money and your western banks wanted to lend it to us because who else would pay such high interest, needing it so badly? Father got his hands on enough of it but what happened, massive inflation, lucky he'd put the money somewhere safe, the Swiss mountains so white from the air like our mountains but the people rich with cattle and clocks and secrets, the American plains yellow with wheat, the green English fields where lords still live in grey stone, all with such safe banks and good bonds and exciting gambles, so as soon as any dollars or pounds come, don't let them go into our mines or our coffee or look for a sea of oil under the jungle, no get it out quickly to the western banks (a little money in cocaine, that's different). Peru leads the way resisting the IMF, refusing to pay the interest, but I don't want to make things difficult for the banks, I prefer to support them, why should my money stay in Peru and suffer? The official closing price yesterday for grade A copper was 878-8.5, three months 900.5-1, final kerb close 901-2. Why bother to send aid so many miles, put it straight into my eurobonds.

Meanwhile the London metal exchange starts quietly trading copper. When JACINTA *finishes speaking the trading reaches its noisy climax.*

ZAC.
There's some enterprising guys around and here's an example.
You know how if you want to get a job in the states you have to give a urine sample?
    (this is to show you're not on drugs.)
There's a company now for a fifty dollar fee
They'll provide you with a guaranteed pure, donated by a churchgoer, bottle of pee.
    (They also plan to market it dehydrated in a packet and you just add water.)
And Aids is making advertisers perplexed
Because it's no longer too good to have your product associated with sex.
But it's a great marketing opportunity.
Like the guys opening up blood banks where you pay to store your own blood in case of an accident and so be guaranteed immunity.
(It's also a great time to buy into rubber.)
Anyone who can buy oranges for ten and sell at eleven in a souk or bazaar
Has the same human nature and can go equally far.

The so-called third world doesn't want our charity or aid.
All they need is the chance to sit down in front of some green screens and trade.
> (They don't have the money, sure, but just so long as they have freedom from communism so they can do it when they do have the money.)

Pictures of starving babies are misleading and patronising.
Because there's plenty of rich people in those countries, it's just the masses that's poor, and Jacinta Condor flew into London and was quite enterprising.
It was the day before Jake Todd was found dead
And the deal was really coming to a head.
Jake was helping us find punters because anyone with too much money and Jake would know them.
You'd just say, Jake, who's in town, what have you got, and he'd bring them in and show them.

ZAC *and* JAKE

JAKE.
Señora Condor has plenty of cash in her coffer.
She owns mountains and her garden's twice
The size of Wales. What's Corman going to offer?

ZAC.
He hopes she'll be able to help support his price.

JAKE.
She's going to need some kind of incentive.

ZAC.
I think she'll find Corman quite inventive.

JAKE.
Zac, while we're alone.
I didn't want to say this on the phone.
I had a visit from a DTI inspector.

ZAC.
Have you done something not quite correct or / what?

JAKE.
Zac, it's no joke. They didn't say too much /
But once they –

ZAC.
Did they mention me?

JAKE.
                              I can't say I don't know
You. / (That doesn't tell them anything, knowing you.)

ZAC.
Great.
Sure, no, of course not.

JAKE.
                              Don't let's pay too much
Attention to it. OK? / If you like I'll go.

ZAC.
                                It could be quite a smash./
    Not just for you.

JAKE.
    I have been making quite a lot of cash.
    When they take your passport you feel surprisingly trapped.
    I didn't know I was so fond of travel.

ZAC.
    You're the kind of loose thread, Jake, that when they pull you the whole fucking City
        could unravel.

JAKE.
    Shall we cancel Condor in case it makes things worse?

ZAC.
    Just don't give them the whole thing giftwrapped.

JAKE.
    I can walk out the door now.

ZAC.
                            OK.

JAKE.
                            I feel –

JAKE.
    What shall I do?

ZAC.
                    Jake, I'm not your nurse.

JAKE.
    Tell me to walk / and I'll walk.

ZAC.
                    And fuck up the deal?

JAKE.
    There might be a bug on the light.

ZAC.
                            Jake, what the hell.
    There might be a microphone under your lapel.
    The City's greed or fear, you've got to choose.

JAKE.
    Greed's been good to me. Fear's a bitch.

ZAC.
    Then be greedy, guy, and let's get this payload home without a hitch.

JAKE.
    I can always hit the straight and narrow tomorrow.

    JACINTA CONDOR *arrives.*

    This is Zac Zackerman you've heard so much about.
    The guy who always knows the latest shout.

ZAC.
How are you enjoying your stay in London, Señora Condor?

JACINTA.
I have been for a walk
In your little saint's park
Where the pelicans eat the pigeons (but I didn't see it).
I have been to the opera (very nice).
I have sold all my copper
For a rather small number of millions.

ZAC.
This is no time to sell copper, the price is lousy.

JAKE.
And when's it ever in season?
She's selling copper she's got to have a reason.

JACINTA.
I lose every quarter,
The cash goes like water,
Is better to close the mine.
I chose very well
The moment to sell,
I benefit from the closures in Surinam because of guerilla activity and also I leak the
    news I am closing my mines, which puts the price up a little, so it is fine.

JAKE.
So you've wiped out your mines? That's telling them who's master.
You must feel like a natural disaster.

ZAC.
Hurricane Jacinta.

JACINTA.
If I keep them Jake I have to be derange.
The Minister of Energy says 'Mining is not dead' –
It brings 45% of our foreign exchange
But a pound of copper won't buy a loaf of bread.
    (Our mining companies lost a hundred million dollars last year, it is the fault of the
IMF. I don't like to suffer.)

JAKE.
The dagos always like to blame the gringos.
I suppose the miners want a revolution.
The most amazing lake full of flamingos –
    (I think that was Peru.)

JACINTA.
How can I support ten thousand people?
When I did they weren't even grateful.
The miners all strike
And do what they like,
They want subsidised food, I say get on your bike.

JAKE.
I didn't know they had bikes, I thought they had llamas, /
And woolly hats and trousers like pyjamas.

ZAC.
>(So are the miners bothering you?

JACINTA.
>You come and protect me?)
>It's really a pity,
>They go to the city (where there's no work)
>Or they sit down outside the mine.
>Growing coca is nice,
>A very good price
>>(Ten to thirty times as much as tea or coffee or cocoa)
>So I think that's going to be fine.

JAKE.
>Great product to grow.
>Peru with its mountains covered in snow.
>You're not giving up all your Peruvian interests?

JACINTA.
>Europe is more interesting. Mr Corman is fascinating.

>Jake, I have asked a friend to this meeting.

ZAC.
>I'm not sure a –

JACINTA.
>You've heard of Nigel Ajibala? /

ZAC.
>I can't say I have.

JAKE.
>Listen, don't cross the señora.

JACINTA.
>I tell you I've caught a
>Big cocoa importer,
>Your deal goes without a hitch.
>His school was at Eton
>Where children are beaten,
>He's a prince and exceedingly rich.

JAKE.
>Any friend of Jacinta
>Will be a good punter.

ZAC.
>So where does he operate?

JACINTA.
>He has connections in

>Ghana and Zambia
>Zaire and Gambia
>But it's here that he likes to invest.
>His enemies are jealous
>Because he's so zealous (and makes so much money)/
>And at home he faces arrest
>>(like the man they tried to kidnap in the trunk?)

JAKE.
> You see, I told you, it's great.

JACINTA.
> Here he comes now. Be cunning.

ZAC.
> I suppose Corman can always meet him.

> NIGEL AJIBALA *arrives.*

JACINTA.
> My friend, Jake Todd, and Mr Zackerman,
> A very considerable American.

JAKE.
> You spend much time in Zambia and Zaire?

NIGEL.
> Yes, but one's mostly based over here.
> Africa induces mild hysteria.
> Terrible situation in Nigeria.
>> (oil earnings down from twenty-five billion dollars to five this year so they're refusing to make their interest payments.)
> And Zaire
> Pays the west a hundred and ninety million more than it receives each year.
> So as the last of several last resorts
> It's cutting its payments to 10% of exports.

JACINTA.
> So the IMF
> Will turn a deaf
> Ear.

NIGEL.
> They've just cut off their payments to Zambia.

ZAC.
> The IMF is not a charity.
> It has to insist on absolute austerity.

NIGEL.
> Absolutely. It can't be namby pamby.
> These countries must accept restricted diets.
> The governments must explain, if there are food riots,
> That paying the western banks is the priority.

JAKE.
> Bob Geldof was a silly cunt.
> He did his charity back to front.
> They should have had the concerts in Zaire
> And shipped the money to banks over here.

ZAC.
> So you're better off out of Africa, I guess.

NIGEL.
>The continent is such a frightful mess.
One's based in London so one's operation
Is on the right side of exploitation.
One thing one learned from one's colonial masters,
One makes money from other people's disasters.

ZAC.
>Señora Condor tells me you might be interested in Corman Enterprise.

>ZAC *takes* NIGEL *aside.*

JAKE.
>You can't completely pull out of Peru.

JACINTA.
>Don't worry, Jake, I don't pull out on you.
I give up all my interests – except the cocaine.
And I keep the houses of course and the aeroplane.
My country is beautiful, Jake, white mountains, jungle greenery.
My people will starve to death among the scenery.
>>(Let them rot, I'm sick of it.)

JAKE.
>So what's the story?

JACINTA.
>The airstrip's rebuilt –
The government feels guilt
So it's always trying to bomb it.
>>(also they try to destroy my processing plants which is deceitful because they dare
not confront the peasants and stop them growing it.)
>And they don't really want
To destroy all the plants.
They are making billions from it (more than all the rest of our exports.)

>To keep Reagan our friend
We have to pretend,
But the US pretends and we know it.
Who likes a coke buzz?
America does.
They stop using it, we won't grow it.

>Till then our one hope
Is the market for dope,
For that we have excellent weather.
I ship the cocaine to Marylou Baines.
I'm glad we are in this together.

JAKE.
>So when can we see some action? Let's get going.

JACINTA.
>I have to get a little cash flowing.
Maybe Mr Corman?

JAKE.
>I'm curious to see Corman, we've never met,
>I'm just a secret compartment in his desk.
>He's very bright so be on your best behaviour.
>He's obsessed with the bid and he'll look on you as a saviour.
>You can push him quite hard, he likes a risk.
>So have you decided what to ask for yet?

JACINTA.
>If I buy or I sell
>I always do well
>So don't worry about it, my pet.
>Whatever I get
>I look after you
>And Corman will too
>I expect.
>Don't be embarrassed, Jake, you're young and greedy, I like to see it.

ZAC and NIGEL rejoin them.

JAKE.
>I was at Eton myself. This is rather a different ballgame.

NIGEL.
>Oh not at all. Did you ever play the wall game?

JAKE and NIGEL talk apart.

ZAC.
>It would be great to see you while you're over here.

JACINTA.
>Maybe we could drink some English beer.
>I have a meeting at eight,
>It won't go on late.
>Maybe at half-past nine?

ZAC.
>No, I don't think . . .
>I'll be stuck with Corman, I can't get out for a drink.
>Eleven's probably fine.

JACINTA.
>I'm having late supper
>With terribly upper-
>class people who buy my plantation.

ZAC.
>And after that?

JACINTA.
>Unfortunately they live in Edinburgh.

ZAC.
>How you getting there?

JACINTA.
>   By helicopter.

ZAC.
I'm beginning to run out of inspiration.

JACINTA.
Breakfast?

ZAC.
Would be great except I have to have breakfast with Corman till this deal goes through.
I suppose I might get away for a minute or two.

JACINTA.
That would be heaven.

ZAC.
Maybe eleven?

JACINTA.
Eleven I see my lawyer.
At twelve –

ZAC.
No, please.

JACINTA.
I see some Japanese,
Just briefly in the hotel foyer.
So we meet for lunch?

ZAC.
I have to be in Paris for lunch. I'll be back by four.

JACINTA.
That's good!

ZAC.
But I have to go straight to Corman.

JACINTA.
What a bore.

ZAC.
Maybe we could . . .

JACINTA.
Dinner tomorrow
Much to my sorrow
I have with some eurobond dealers.

ZAC.
Cancel it.

JACINTA.
Business.

ZAC.
Shit.

JACINTA.
Afterward?

ZAC.
> Bliss.
> No, hang on a minute.
> I have as a guest a
> Major investor,
> I have to put out some feelers.
> (The only time he can meet me is after a show.)
> I guess I might be through by 1 a.m.

JACINTA.
> Zac, I could cry,
> There's a nightclub I buy,
> And really I must talk to them.
> So maybe next morning
> You give me a ring?

ZAC.
> Maybe I can get out of breakfast with Corman, I'll call you first thing.

JACINTA.
> Which day?

ZAC.
> Tomorrow.

> NIGEL *and* JAKE.

NIGEL.
> If you fancy a wolfhound I'll let you have a pup.

JAKE.
> If I'm down in Wiltshire I'll certainly look you up.

> ZAC *takes* JAKE *aside.*

JACINTA (*to* NIGEL).
> That went very well.
> They can't possibly tell
> You live in one room in a rundown hotel.

> I'll buy you a silk shirt in Jermyn Street.

> ZAC *and* JAKE.

ZAC.
> You've not met Corman before, had you better split?
> There may be a good time to meet him but is this it?
> If you've actually spoken it gets us in more deep –

JAKE.
> What the hell, Zac. Hang for a sheep.

ZAC *joins* CORMAN *and* ETHERINGTON *in* CORMAN's *office.*

CORMAN.
  Cup of coffee someone. I'm going mental.
  So we get these people involved in distribution,
  Or supply, whatever, and they make a contribution?

ZAC.
  Their involvement should look kind of coincidental.

CORMAN.
  Look what? Zac, don't you start talking sin,
  It'll look terrific. Show the buggers in.

  NIGEL, JACINTA *and* JAKE *come into* CORMAN's *office.*

ZAC.
  Señora Condor. Mr Ajibala.

CORMAN.
  And this must be the infamous Jake Todd.
  I'd begun to think you were a bit like God –
  You make things happen but you don't exist.
  Etherington, don't look as if you smell something burning.
  This is Jake Todd, our invisible earning.

ETHERINGTON.
  How do you do, Mr Todd. Extremely glad.

JAKE.
  You're really so looked up to by my dad.

CORMAN.
  OK, let's skip the introductions.
  How do you do. Let's get on with the ructions.
  What's the idea?

NIGEL.
  Albion seems an excellent investment
  Especially under your expert control.
  I assure you that the stag is not my role.
  I'm talking about a long term commitment.

CORMAN.
  So you'd have the company's interests at heart?

NIGEL.
  I'd certainly be glad to play my part.
  I can't imagine why anyone bothers with water
  When Albion produces so many delicious drinks.
  Orange, coffee, chocolate / with cream –

CORMAN.
  I think the product stinks.
  Cocoa? you're a cocoa importer?
  I know fuckall about the cocoa bean.
  Buy the company first and run it later.

NIGEL.
>The London market suits the speculator.
>You really have to know your way around.
>And excellent bargains can be made.

CORMAN.
>You've wide experience have you in the trade?

NIGEL.
>The only job I haven't done is peasant
>Who grows the stuff, which wouldn't be so pleasant.

CORMAN.
>So what's the story with cocoa –
>Anyone know?
>Are Albion having to pay through the nose?

NIGEL.
>There's mistrust between the countries where it grows
>And countries like this where we consume.
>Cocoa is very far from having a boom.
>A new agreement has just been implemented.

ZAC.
>(Hell of a lot of wrangling about the buffer stock.)

NIGEL.
>This has driven the price up a little but it's well below the price at which buffer stock
>   buying is permitted,
>And 18% down on a year ago.
>We consumers are holding the price low.

CORMAN.
>So how can you give me a better price than your rivals?

NIGEL.
>Because options and futures are more important than physicals
>(In today's market following an unchanged opening futures rallied £15 during the
>   afternoon before trade profit taking pared the gains on the closing call. With
>   producers withdrawn physical interest was restricted to forward / consumer
>   offtake –)

JAKE.
>He buys a forward contract, sells it later,
>And every time he's making money off it.

ZAC.
>And you get the benefit of the profit.

JACINTA.
>It's thrilling to watch such a skilful operator.

CORMAN.
>And funny business with import licences, Mr Ajibala? Don't answer that.
>Right Zac, let's put cocoa on the back burner.
>It looks as if it's a nice little earner.
>And you Señora? Are you full of beans?
>I suppose you want to sell me some caffeine?

JACINTA.
Coffee's no joke,
It makes me go broke,
No, my interest is distribution –

CORMAN.
I spent a good weekend once in Caracas.
You don't by any chance play the maracas?

JACINTA.
I'm here to do business, Mr Corman.
I wish to obtain an exclusive franchise.

CORMAN.
Señoritas in Brazil have beautiful eyes. /

ZAC.
Cut it out, Corman.

JACINTA.
Mr Corman, you appreciate my country's spirit.
I appreciate your company's products and I wish to sell it in Peru, Brazil, Argentina,
    Venezuela and Chile.

ZAC.
This could very probably be arranged.

CORMAN.
Zackerman, I hope you haven't changed.

ZAC.
The proposal has considerable merit.

CORMAN.
You wouldn't be suggesting something silly?
Can you tell me anything good the present distributors did?

ZAC.
No, they've shown no interest at all in your bid.

CORMAN.
That's too bad.
I think we may be in business, Señora.

JACINTA.
If you want to set up
Debt for equity swap
And have Albion plants in Peru
It's a way that we get
To sell some of our debt.
I ask you, what else can we do?
Better than selling copper.

CORMAN.
Zac, do I want to invest in South America?

ZAC.
South American companies will swap their debt
For dollars you invest in their country, which means you get

> Say a hundred million dollars of equity
> Paid by the government in local currency
> And you've only got to hand over seventy.
> It gives you a great advantage over the locals.

JACINTA.
> Also you could help to build my hospitals.
> I have one for sick and hungry men and women,
> One for poor drug-addicted children.
> I visit and hold the hands of the poor peopole.

CORMAN.
> This is all extremely admirable,
> Don't you think so, Etherington? (*To* JACINTA.) If you'll excuse us.

CORMAN *takes* ZAC *and* ETHERINGTON *aside.*

> Is this wise?
> Hospitals, she's simply trying to use us.
> Every penny would go in her own pocket.
> Everything she looks at I want to lock it.
> You can't help admiring the way she tries.
> Etherington?

ETHERINGTON.
> I'm afraid I can't advise.
> Questions of supply and distribution
> For Albion after you make the acquisition
> Are matters of internal management,
> So naturally, I haven't liked to listen. /
> I really don't feel qualified to comment.

CORMAN.
> Do you want the money for the deal or not?
> Zac?

ZAC.
> Swapping debt might come in handy later.
> I agree the hospitals / are just a scam.

CORMAN.
> Hospitals! what does she think I am?

ZAC.
> So we buy his cocoa, give her the franchise and get out the calculator.

CORMAN.
> They have got serious money?

ZAC.
> Jake recommends / them.

CORMAN.
> That boy's got very interesting friends.
> Let's keep them sweet.

CORMAN *returns to others.*

I'd be delighted to make a small contribution
To your hospital, Señora. The distribution
Franchise would of course be contingent
On my acquiring Albion.

JACINTA.
>I know the arrangement.
If you get it, I get it. I help you get it.

CORMAN.
And Mr Ajibala.
I'm most impressed. As Albion's sole supplier /
Of cocoa?

NIGEL.
I would feel it my duty to acquire /
An interest in the company.

CORMAN.
I think a change of supplier is probably indicated,
Don't you, Zac?
Right, you can both discuss the exact sum
With my banker here, Mr Zackerman.

NIGEL.
There's a small problem.
I was hoping to buy five-million poundsworth of Albion stock but I have a holdup in
cash liquidity.

CORMAN.
That is a problem.

NIGEL.
I suppose it is a matter of some urgency?
If my involvement could be postponed, ten days, or eight?

CORMAN.
That's too late.

NIGEL.
If I had an extra two million now a five million purchase could be made by several
small companies under various names registered in various places not traceable to
anyone alive.

ZAC.
Maybe if he buys three million now / and two –

CORMAN.
>Zac, I want five. Five!

NIGEL.
I don't have five at my immediate disposal.

CORMAN.
Mr Ajibala, if you're happy with my proposal / about the cocoa

NIGEL.
Perfectly.

CORMAN.
>   I could make a downpayment of two million in advance.
>   (We're going to need a hell of a lot of cocoa beans.)

NIGEL.
>   That way nothing would be left to chance.

CORMAN.
>   Zackerman will write a cheque.
>   And Señora Condor, if you see my lawyer.

JACINTA.
>   The deal is exciting,
>   I get it in writing?

CORMAN.
>   I can't be bothered with all these trivialities.
>   We've got the money. Fuck the personalities.
>   Etherington will see you all right for stock.

>   CORMAN *and* ETHERINGTON *leave, followed by* ZAC.

ZACKERMAN.
>   I'll call you first thing.

JACINTA, NIGEL *and* JAKE.

NIGEL.
>   I've got the money! / Two million!

JACINTA.
>   For Albion?

NIGEL.
>   I want a better return,
>   Albion won't earn,

JACINTA.
>   Put up your stake,
>   Get it doubled / by Jake.

NIGEL.
>   Doubled?

JACINTA.
>   He's a good dealer, let him play with it.

JAKE.
>   No problem. Give me a week.

NIGEL.
>   I'll go and get the cheque from Zackerman.

>   NIGEL *goes.*

JACINTA.
>   Two million. What are you going to do?

JAKE.
>I thought I might invest it in Peru.

>JACINTA *phones* MARYLOU BAINES.

JACINTA.
>Hello? Marylou?
>Four million, repeat four,
>Arrives Thursday, the usual way.

MARYLOU.
>But the CIA
>Won't help it through
>Unless we agree to give /
>>another 10% to the Contras.

JACINTA.
>But Marylou, already we pay –

MARYLOU.
>I don't think we have an alternative.

JACINTA.
>I expect an increase in what I get from you.

MARYLOU.
>No problem. The guys who use it can easily meet
>A rise in the street price because the street is Wall Street.

JACINTA.
>So how's the weather?

MARYLOU.
>I haven't looked.

During the above, ZAC *looks in just for this exchange with* JAKE.

ZAC.
>Good work, Jake.

JAKE.
>I'd be OK if my hands didn't shake.

>JACINTA *comes off the phone.*

JACINTA.
>Good work, Jake. The franchise I got from Corman – what a pig –
>I sell of course to some American.
>You will arrange it, no wonder I am so fond,
>And I put the money in a delicious Eurobond,
>Yumyum.
>I think that is all.
>One more phone call,
>Then I go see Biddulph, the white knight –
>But you don't mention this to Zac, all right?

JAKE.
>This deal's not enough?

JACINTA.
What is enough?

Don't worry, Jake, you're making it.

Just keep on, taking and taking and taking it.

JAKE.

I do.

JACINTA *phones a shop.*

JACINTA.

I like to order a tree. Maybe twenty feet tall. Fig, walnut, banyan? Lemon, yes that's
  sweet.

Send it please to Zac Zackerman, Klein Merrick, and a card saying 'to Zac with love
  from Jacinta until we meet.'

DUCKETT *and* BIDDULPH. BIDDULPH *has a newspaper.*

BIDDULPH.

Now Duckett, your image gets better and better.

Have you seen this letter?

DUCKETT.
No, show me the letter.

BIDDULPH.

MPs of all parties and union leaders,

Teachers and lawyers and ordinary readers

All hope you'll succeed

DUCKETT.
Oh let's have a read.

BIDDULPH.

In stopping the raider who just wants a profit.

DUCKETT.

But we want a profit.

BIDDULPH.
We will make a profit.

But at the right time and in the right place,

With a smile on our very acceptable face.

You do so much good, you give so much enjoyment –

DUCKETT.

Youth unemployment.

BIDDULPH.
Yes, youth unemployment,

Swimming pools, pensioners, toy libraries, art –

DUCKETT.

What's this about art?

BIDDULPH.
You don't give a fart,

I know it, they know it, you just mustn't show it,
We're doing so well, Duckett, don't you dare blow it.
You've commissioned a mural called Urban and Rural,
It's sixty feet high –

DUCKETT.
                    I've commissioned a mural?

BIDDULPH.
And tomorrow you're joining the scouts for a hike.

DUCKETT.
         I'm not sure I like –

BIDDULPH.
                    You go for a hike.
Your picture will be on the front of the Mail.
And we really can't fail.

DUCKETT.
                    You're sure we can't fail?
Sometimes I dream that I'll end up in jail.

BIDDULPH.
But you've done nothing wrong, you're an innocent victim,
Corman's the villain, you'll see when we've licked him.
He's sure to be up to some terrible schemes.

DUCKETT.
         I just have bad dreams.

BIDDULPH.
                    Well don't have bad dreams.

DUCKETT.
         I've done nothing wrong, I'm an innocent victim.

BIDDULPH.
And Corman will lose because we have tricked him.

Now we're meeting Señora Condor.
What the hell's she want I wonder.

         JACINTA CONDOR *arrives.*

JACINTA.
         Mr Duckett. Miss Biddulph. As a major shareholder I have been wondering whether I
         should accept Corman's offer.

BIDDULPH.
         You don't want to do that Señora Condor.

JACINTA.
         I was hoping you could help me to make up my mind. I don't know how much you know
         about my country.

BIDDULPH.
         It's really absurd, from what I have heard,
         You bear an intolerable burden of debt.

JACINTA.
> My country is poor, it can't stand much more,
> I really can see no solution just yet.
> When I wish to borrow, much to my sorrow,
> The banks here in Britain are overextended.

BIDDULPH.
> I think they might lend a small sum to a friend,
> And we hope this sad period is very soon ended.

JACINTA.
> You think your bank will lend me money?

BIDDULPH.
> I think if I explain the special circumstances it could probably be arranged.

JACINTA.
> Señora Biddulph
> You are pleased with yourself
> And certainly so you ought.
> And ah Señor Duckett
> You don't know your luck, it
> Is now my decision you get my support.

DUCKETT.
> We get her support?

BIDDULPH.
>   Just as we ought.

DUCKETT.
> I sometimes have dreams that I'll end up in court.

JACINTA.
> And now do you think it is time for a drink?

BIDDULPH.
> Time for a drink!

DUCKETT.
>   What do you think, Biddulph?

BIDDULPH.
> I'm telling you, Duckett.
> I begin to think fuck it.
> Pull yourself together.

MERRISON *and* MARYLOU BAINES *at* MARYLOU'*s office in New York.*

MERRISON.
> So I've had three years pretty much in the wilderness.
> I've had a great time skiing with my kids.
> I've bred Tennessee walking horses. But I guess
> Banking's in my blood. I miss the bids,
> I miss the late nights, I miss the gambles.
> So now I've got my own operation.

I can't forgive Durkfeld for the shambles
He's made of Klein Merrick. A great nation
Needs great entrepreneurs, not black plastic
And grey lino and guys in polyester.
    (I just bought a Matisse for seven million dollars,
    could have hung in the boardroom.)

MARYLOU.
I guess the old wound's beginning to fester.
It's about time you did something drastic.
Go for it, Jack. Why don't you sabotage
Durkfeld's deals? I've got a lot of stocks
Coming and going here in arbitrage
Should enable you to give him a few knocks.

MERRISON.
He's got his fingers in a lot of pies.

MARYLOU.
In the UK there's Corman Enterprise.

MERRISON.
You think I should step in as a white knight?

MARYLOU.
No, that's already happening all right.
Wouldn't it be far wittier to make
Corman himself a target?

MERRISON.
                        I'll buy a stake
In Corman straight away. I'll get some little
Nogood company run by a real punk
To take it over with a lot of junk.
I'd really like to see Durkfeld in hospital.
Do you happen to have any Corman stock available?

MARYLOU.
Yes, I kind of thought it might be saleable.
How much do you want?

MERRISON.
How much have you got?

MARYLOU.
Let's talk to TK.

MERRISON *goes.*

TK? Sell Mr Merrison all the Corman we've got.
And buy all you can get straight away.
He'll give us a good price and take the lot.

TK.
OK.

SCILLA *and* GRIMES *playing Pass the Pigs.*

SCILLA.
    Grimes and I were having a glass of poo and playing Pass the Pig,
    Where you throw little pigs like dice. It's a good way to unwind
    Because when trading stops you don't know what to do with your mind.

GRIMES.
    Trotter!

SCILLA.
    Except my mind was also full of Jake and how he'd been up to something big.

GRIMES.
    Razorback, snouter. Fucking pig out.
    I knew Jake was up to something but I'd never have guessed that was what it was about.

SCILLA.
    He might have made a million. Trotter. Razorback.

GRIMES.
    Marylou Baines! And he's in on it somehow, Zac.
    Did he leave a will?

SCILLA.
                    I don't know.

GRIMES.
                            Trotter, snouter.
    Fucking nuisance if he's died without a
    Will, / fucking lawyers

SCILLA.
                    Daddy and I are next of kin.

GRIMES.
    Will you marry me?

SCILLA.
                    Leave it out Grimes.

GRIMES.
    Double snouter. I think I'm going to win.
    I once threw double snouter three times.

SCILLA.
    Are we playing a pound a point?

GRIMES.
                            Snouter, trotter.
    There's the money he's made already. There's a lot o'
    Money still owing him, bound to be,
    And why can't that be collected by you and me?
    It's just a matter of tracing his contacts, innit.
    They'll want him replacing. / Snouter!

SCILLA.
                            You'll pig out in a minute.
    There's someone who killed him.

GRIMES.
                                    Risks are there to be taken.
    Trotter, jowler. Fuckit, makin' bacon.
    Do I lose all my points for the whole game?

SCILLA.
    Yes, Grimes, isn't it a shame.
    And I've got forty-five. Trotter, fifty. / Snouter, sixty. Double razorback, eighty. Hell,
        I've pigged out. Back to forty-five.

GRIMES.
    I'd have some questions for Jake if he was alive.
    What about your old man?

SCILLA.
                                Denies he got a single tip.

GRIMES.
    I bet he knows more / than he lets on.

SCILLA.
                            He'll be so pissed by now he might let something slip.

GRIMES.
    He may know where Jake stashed the loot.

SCILLA.
    Let's go round there now and put in the boot.
    Really, this morning he couldn't have been fouler.
    Let's drive / there now.

GRIMES.
                        Double leaning jowler!
    Double leaning jowler as I live and breathe!

SCILLA.
    He's so two-faced you don't know what to believe.
    We'll make him talk.

GRIMES.
    I'm winning! Double fucking leaning jowler!

SCILLA.
    Bring the pigs.

GREVILLE *and* FROSBY at GREVILLE's *house. Drinking.*

GREVILLE.
    It's times like this you need an old friend.
    We haven't seen each other for a while,
    I blame myself but know that in the end
    It's only you that travels that last mile.
    It helps so much to have someone I'm fond
    Of here to sit and drink and share my grief.
    There's no one else I'm sure his word's his bond.
    Talking things over gives me such relief.

FROSBY.
Greville, there's something –

GREVILLE.
Poor Jake. You knew him as a little lad.
Remember the wooden soldier you once made him?

FROSBY.
Greville, there's something –

GREVILLE.
He wasn't really bad.
Some bastard whizzkid probably betrayed him.
Poor Jakey, how could anybody sell you?

FROSBY.
Greville, there's something that I ought to tell you.

SCILLA *and* GRIMES *arrive.*

SCILLA.
Daddy!

GREVILLE.
Scilla!

SCILLA.
Grimes, a colleague. My dad. Mr Frosby.

GRIMES.
Nice place you've got. High ceilings. Plenty of headroom.
Room for a chandelier. How many bedrooms?

GREVILLE.
Six, actually, now that you come to mention –

GRIMES.
That's all right. I could always build an extension.

GREVILLE.
It's not for sale.

GRIMES.
No, I was just thinking.
I'd give you half a million.

GREVILLE.
What are you drinking?

SCILLA.
Daddy. Tell me the truth if you're sober en –
ough to talk properly. About Jake.

GRIMES.
I'd get an alsatian and a doberman.

GREVILLE.
Darling, I think you're making a mistake.

SCILLA.
Do I know more than you? Marylou Baines.
Yes?

GREVILLE.
>Now Scilla –

SCILLA.
>>Don't think you can smile a
>Lot and not tell me. Ill gotten gains,
>Right? Millions!

GRIMES.
>>I'll get a rotweiller.

SCILLA.
>And nobody told me.

GREVILLE.
>>I know nothing about –

SCILLA.
>Nothing?

GREVILLE.
>>Scilla, there's no need to shout.
>Of course my son would make the odd suggestion –

SCILLA.
>Where's his money.

GREVILLE.
>>But there's no question –
>Marylou Baines?

GRIMES.
>>A rotweiller's a killer.

SCILLA.
>What about me?

GREVILLE.
>>I protected you, Scilla.
>It's bad enough to see a woman get work
>Without her being part of an old boy network.

SCILLA.
>Fuck off. I want my share.

GREVILLE.
>>Your share of what?
>Daddy's always given you all he's got.
>My little girl! Jake seems to have been much bigger
>Than poor old daddy knew. If it's as you say,
>If we're really dealing with a six nought figure.
>Where the hell's he hidden it away?

GRIMES.
>Don't piss about. We haven't got all day.
>Who's his solicitor?

GREVILLE.
>>I'm afraid I don't –

GRIMES.
Who's his accountant?

GREVILLE.
In any case I won't –

FROSBY.
Who is this? An awful lout.

GRIMES.
If he really don't know we should get back.

FROSBY.
Ordering everyone about.

GRIMES.
It might be more use talking to Zac.

SCILLA.
If you're holding out on me daddy you'll be sorry.

GRIMES.
We'll have your feet run over by a lorry.

FROSBY.
Who is this horrible young vandal?
I don't need to know his name.
Responsible for all the scandal.
He's the one you ought to blame.

GRIMES.
You've all been coining it for years.

FROSBY.
My lovely city's sadly changed.
Sic transit gloria! Glory passes!
Any wonder I'm deranged,
Surrounded by the criminal classes.

GRIMES.
You've all been coining it for years.
All you fuckwits in the City.
It just don't look quite so pretty,
All the cunning little jobs,
When you see them done by yobs.

FROSBY.
He's the one you ought to blame.

GRIMES.
We're only doing just the same
All you bastards always done.
New faces in your old square mile,
Making money with a smile,
Just as clever, just as vile.

GREVILLE.
No, he's right, you killed my son.

GRIMES.
>All your lives you've been in clover,
>Fucking everybody over,
>You just don't like to see us at it.

GREVILLE.
>Scilla, I forbid you to associate with this oik.

SCILLA.
>Daddy, you're trading like a cunt.
>This is a waste of time. I'm going to see Corman again.

GREVILLE.
>Scilla, wait, if you find out about Jake's money –

SCILLA.
>Don't worry, I won't tell you, I'll protect you.

GREVILLE.
>Scilla –

GRIMES.
>If you want to sell the house I can pay cash.

SCILLA and GRIMES leave.

GREVILLE.
>Because of yobs like him my Jake was led astray.
>If it wasn't for that bastard he'd be alive today.
>It's times like this you need an old friend –

FROSBY.
>Greville.
>It's me that told the DTI.
>I can't remember why.
>It didn't occur to me he'd die.

ZAC

ZAC.
>That afternoon things were going from bad to worse.
>Jake was dead and I'd just as soon it was me they'd taken off in a hearse.
>I'd just discovered Jacinta and Ajibala were no fucking help at all,
>And I find Scilla hanging about in the hall.

ZAC and SCILLA outside CORMAN's office.

SCILLA.
>Zac, I want to see Corman. Get me in.

ZAC.
>Don't talk to me. We may not even win.
>Jacinta Condor's supporting Biddulph which may wreck
>The whole deal, and Nigel Ajibala's done god knows what with a two million pound
>>cheque.

SCILLA.
>Jacinta Condor? Nigel Ajibala?

ZAC.
>I've got to get this sorted / before Corman finds out.

SCILLA.
>But they were in Jake's diary.

ZAC.
>   Scilla, don't shout.

SCILLA.
>Would either of them be likely to kill
>Jake? Or more important still
>Could they tell me about his bank account?
>Which bank is it in? / And what's the total amount?

ZAC.
>They've kicked this dog of a deal when I hoped they'd pat it. /
>I've got to find them.

SCILLA.
>And if it's in a numbered Swiss account, Zac, how do I get at it?

ZAC goes. MELISSA, a model, enters.

SCILLA.
>Are you going to see Mr Corman?

MELISSA.
>   I don't know his name.
>I'm having a picture taken. The PR
>Consultant is in there with him, she's called Dolcie Starr.
>Last time I did a job like this the bastard put his hand on my crutch.
>I was ready to walk out, I said, 'What's your game?'
>I hope nothing like that –

SCILLA.
>Can I go instead of you?

MELISSA.
>   How much?

CORMAN *and* DOLCIE STARR, *a PR consultant.*

CORMAN.
>My image is atrocious. 'Profiteering.'
>'Decline of British Industry.' 'Robber gangs.'
>There's even a cartoon here where I'm leering
>At an innocent girl called Albion and I've got fangs.
>I want to be seen as Albion's Mr Right.
>I need to be transformed overnight.
>Can you make me look as good as Duckett?

STARR.
No, I'm afraid he's completely cornered the market
In fatherly, blue-eyed, babies, workers' friend,
Someone on whom the CBI can depend –

CORMAN.
I'm all that.

STARR.
No, you're none of that.

CORMAN.
Shit.

STARR.
Cheer up, Corman, you're the opposite.

CORMAN.
Then what am I paying you good money for?

STARR.
Let Duckett be good. And a bore.
Then you can be bad. And glamorous.
You'll have top billing by tonight.
Everyone loves a villain if he's handled right. /
Bad has connotations of amorous.

CORMAN.
Bad and glamorous?

STARR.
Two dimensions, spiritual and physical. First, spiritual.

CORMAN.
That's Duckett's area. He's a lay preacher. /
You don't want me to be a Moslem?

STARR.
No, secular spiritual. Arts. For you to reach a
Wide audience it's absolutely essential /
You sponsor

CORMAN.
Duckett sponsors arts.

STARR.
He sponsors provincial
Orchestras. You need the National
Theatre for power, opera for decadence,
String quartets bearing your name for sensitivity and elegance,
And a fringe show with bad language for a thrill.
That should take care of the spiritual.
Now the physical. It's a pity you haven't a yacht.

CORMAN.
I'll buy one now.

STARR.
No, we'll work with what we've got.
I do recommend a sex scandal.

CORMAN.
> Sex scandal? / That's the last thing –

STARR.
> Will you let me handle this?
> You think because you're already scandalous /
> In the financial –

CORMAN.
> I don't want –

STARR.
> But that's the point. Fight scandal with scandal.
> We provide a young girl who'll say you did it eight times a night.
> Your wife is standing by you, so that's all right. /

CORMAN.
> (I'm not married.)

STARR.
> There could be a suggestion the girl might take her life –
> If necessary we provide the wife.

CORMAN.
> I'm not sure –

STARR.
> There's ugly greedy and sexy greedy, you dope.
> At the moment you're ugly which is no hope.
> If you stay ugly, god knows what your fate is.
> But sexy greedy *is* the late eighties.

CORMAN.
> What about Aids? I thought sexy was out.

STARR.
> The more you don't do it, the more it's fun to read about.
> We might have you make a statement about taking care.
> Wicked and responsible, the perfect chair/man.

CORMAN.
> I don't think I –

STARR.
> We can take the pictures straightaway. / Melissa!

CORMAN.
> Pictures?

STARR.
> You don't have to do a thing, not even kiss her.

SCILLA *comes in.*

SCILLA.
> Melissa's ill. I'm Scilla, the replacement.

STARR.
> You need to stand more adjacent.

CORMAN.
I can't stop working while you take pictures. Zac!
Where the fuck's he gone and why isn't he back?

He recognises SCILLA.

You again?

SCILLA *and* CORMAN *talk while* STARR *takes photographs.*

SCILLA.
I've important news for you about Albion,
If you'll tell me more about Jake.

CORMAN.
What news?

SCILLA.
Jacinta Condor?

CORMAN.
What about her?

SCILLA.
How much did he make?

STARR.
Please look fonder.

SCILLA.
How much did you pay him?

CORMAN.
Two hundred grand.

SCILLA.
What did he do with it?

STARR.
If you took her hand.

CORMAN.
What about the señora?

SCILLA.
She's supporting Biddulph's bid.

STARR.
Could you be more a-
ffectionate – keep still please. Please smile. Smile, kid.

CORMAN.
I'll kill the bitch. /
I knew there was something funny.

SCILLA.
He was so fucking rich.
Who else gave him money?

CORMAN.
What else? Is that the lot?

SCILLA.
Ajibala.

CORMAN.
What? what?

SCILLA.
More about Jake, or I won't say a word.

CORMAN.
I could name six companies he's dealt with, four merchant banks and two MPs and
that's only what I've heard.
Your brother was widely respected in the City.
Now what about Ajibala? have some pity.

SCILLA.
I'll tell you about him for a small fee.
Three companies, two banks and one MP.

CORMAN *whispers to* SCILLA. STARR *snaps enthusiastically.*

STARR.
That's the way. That's what we like to see.
Look as if you're having a lot of fun.
We'll have the front page story of the *Sun.*

SCILLA.
Ajibala's gone off with the two million you gave him.

CORMAN.
Not bought my stock? There's nothing going to save him. Zac!

He realises about the pictures.

CORMAN.
Hang on a minute, you can't use these, this girl is the sister of the dead whizzkid in
today's papers.

STARR.
And that's a scandal with which you've got no connection?

CORMAN.
No, that's the scandal where there is a connection but I don't want it known, I just want
to be connected with the fictitious scandal where I've got a permanent erection.
(Eight times a night? Maybe four, let's be plausible.)

STARR.
But we can't let the whole story escape us.
This other scandal's a high-profile thriller.
Terrific pictures. / What's your name? Scilla?

CORMAN.
No, please –

SCILLA.
What's this about eight times a night?

STARR.
You make a statement to the press saying –

SCILLA.
>Right. Keep paying or I'll agree.
>Three companies.

>CORMAN *whispers to* SCILLA.

>Two banks.

>CORMAN *whispers.*

>One MP.

>CORMAN *whispers.*

SCILLA.
>I've never seen Mr Corman before.
>From what I do see he's an awful bore.

CORMAN.
>Great. More! more! Don't skimp.

SCILLA.
>He's physically repellant. What a wimp.

STARR.
>OK OK, I get it. What duplicity.
>Why don't you people appreciate publicity?
>You've wasted a lot of film. Where's Melissa?

>STARR *leaves.*

CORMAN.
>Do you want a job? Most of the people who work for me are mentally defective.

SCILLA.
>Maybe later when I've finished being a detective.

CORMAN.
>Zac! Etherington!
>I want blood. What the fuck's going on?

>ZAC *comes in followed by* NIGEL AJIBALA.

ZAC.
>Hold on, I've got Ajibala right here.

CORMAN.
>Where's my money? You'd better start talking fast.
>You can stick your cocoa beans up your arse.
>Where's my two million pounds?

NIGEL.
>I'm delighted to have this opportunity
>Of explaining how by judicious speculation
>I plan to increase the sum that you gave me so that I can buy even more shares in support
>>of your acquisition.
>I think I may certainly say with impunity /
>That when you

>ETHERINGTON *comes in with* GREVETT, *a DTI inspector.*

CORMAN.
Ajibala, I've been tricked.
I gave you two million pounds / on the strict
Understanding that you'd –

ETHERINGTON.
Mr Corman. Mr Corman. Mr Corman.

GREVETT.
Do finish your sentence, Mr Corman.

CORMAN.
What's going on? Who the hell's this?
Who let him in? Sack the receptionist.

GREVETT.
I identified myself to your receptionist
As Grevett from the Department of Trade and Industry. /
People don't usually refuse to see me.

CORMAN.
Very nice to meet you, Mr Grevett.

ETHERINGTON.
I assured Mr Grevett we'd be delighted to assist
With his inquiries in any way we could. /
We know the DTI is a force for good.

CORMAN.
Delighted.

GREVETT.
What was that about two million pounds?

ETHERINGTON.
I thought it might interest you, because it sounds /
Unusual, but in fact –

CORMAN.
What was it, Zac?

ZAC.
Mr Corman is paying Klein Merrick, the bank I work for, two million pounds for
    advisory /
Services

ETHERINGTON.
           The sum's derisory /
Considering the immense –

GREVETT.
I believed he was addressing this gentleman?

ETHERINGTON.
                                    By no means.

CORMAN.
Mr Ajibala, who supplies our cocoa beans.

GREVETT.
So the sum in question was to do with the cocoa trade?

ZAC *and* ETHERINGTON.
>No.

CORMAN.
>Yes. That is no, but we have made
>Some arrangements to do with cocoa which were being discussed.

ETHERINGTON.
>But the two million pounds was a payment to Klein.

ZAC.
>Yes, that side of the business is all mine.

GREVETT.
>Mr Ajibala, you can confirm I trust
>That you never received the sum of two million?

NIGEL.
>I only wish I had.

>*All laugh except* GREVETT.

GREVETT.
>The suggestion seems to cause you some amusement.
>I have to establish you see that no inducement
>Financial or otherwise was offered by Mr Corman
>To buy stock to help support his price.

NIGEL.
>Two million pounds would be extremely nice.
>But no, Mr Grevett, I assure you.
>An account of the cocoa trade would only bore you.

GREVETT.
>And you Mr Corman would confirm – ?

CORMAN.
>Absolutely.

GREVETT.
>It sounded as if you were asking him to return
>Two million pounds. I must have misunderstood.
>You weren't asking – ?

CORMAN.
>No, no no, why should I?
>I never gave him a two million pound cheque.

NIGEL.
>So naturally he can't ask for it back.
>I must be going. I've meetings to attend.
>Good afternoon, Mr Corman.

CORMAN.
>Wait.

GREVETT.
>What?

CORMAN.
>Nothing.

SCILLA *waylays* NIGEL *on his way out.*

SCILLA.
I've got to talk to you. You were a friend
Of my brother Jake.

NIGEL.
Who? I never met him.

SCILLA.
It seems to be very easy to forget him.
Do you owe him money?

NIGEL.
This is crazier and crazier.
If you'll excuse me I have a very important meeting about cocoa stocks in Malaysia.

NIGEL AJIBALA *leaves.*

GREVETT.
Does the name Jake Todd ring a bell?

CORMAN.
No. Oh yes, in the paper. Most unfortunate.
(I hope the stupid bastard rots in hell.)

GREVETT.
Not someone with whom you were personally acquainted?

CORMAN.
No, not at all. He seems to have been tainted /
By allegations of –

GREVETT.
I don't wish to be importunate,
But I was wondering if it would be possible for me to cast an eye
Over any papers relating to your interest in Albion, just a formality.

CORMAN.
This way.

GREVETT.
Your involvement, Mrs Etherington, naturally goes a long way to reassure us of the
transaction's total legality.

ETHERINGTON.
There could of course be aspects of which I wasn't aware because my participation
wasn't required.

CORMAN.
Etherington, you're fired.

GREVETT *and* ETHERINGTON *leave.*

CORMAN.
We'll give him a pile of papers ten feet high
And keep him busy till after the deal's completed.
Fuck the DTI, Zac, I refuse to be defeated.
I don't care if I go to jail, I'll win whatever the cost.
They may say I'm a bastard but they'll never say I lost.

ZAC.
> Corman, there's one thing.
> Gleason called and said he's seeing Lear at the National.
> Could you meet him and have a word at the interval.
> I don't know why you're being asked to meet a government minister,
> I hope it's nothing sinister.
> But when the government asks you for a date, you don't stand them up.

CORMAN.
> Fuck.

CORMAN *leaves.* ZAC *and* SCILLA *alone.*

ZAC.
> Whether we'll get away with this is anybody's guess.
>> (My guess is no.)
> And to think Jacinta Condor – / god, what an awful mess.

SCILLA.
> She knew Jake, didn't she? Ajibala denied it.

ZAC.
> He's the key to all the deals, of course they're going to hide it.

SCILLA.
> I want to meet them.

ZAC.
>> Scilla, we all have to lie low.

SCILLA.
> I want to meet all his contacts because someone's going to know where / his money is.

ZAC.
> It'll be in a nominee company, and god knows where, no one except maybe Marylou
> Baines might know.

SCILLA.
> Then I'll go and see Marylou Baines. / She's the one who made him.

ZAC.
> No Scilla, I didn't mean –

SCILLA.
> Yes, she'll know where his money is because she'll know how she paid him.
> Do you think she owes him money? / Maybe I could collect.

ZAC.
> Scilla –

SCILLA.
>> I'll go to New York / tonight.

ZAC.
> Scilla, we must keep out of the news.
> If you're going to be stupid I'll call Marylou and warn her and she'll refuse –

SCILLA.
> How much does Mr Grevett of the DTI suspect?
> I could go and have a word / with him

ZAC.
> Scilla, don't be absurd.

SCILLA.
> I could have my picture in the papers
> With Corman alleging all kinds of capers /
> And linking him publicly with bad Jake Todd

ZAC.
> Scilla, you wouldn't. God.

SCILLA.
> So call Marylou Baines and tell her I'm on my way to Heathrow and she's to see me. Do it.

ZAC.
> At least you'll be out of England.

SCILLA.
> I'll send you a postcard.

ZAC.
> Scilla, I thought you were some kind of English rose.

SCILLA.
> Go stick the thorns up your nose, bozo.

> SCILLA *goes*.

ZAC.
> Somewhere along the line I really blew it.

MERRISON *and* SOAT, *President of Missouri Gumballs, at a drugstore in Missouri.*

MERRISON.
> So how would you like to acquire a multinational?

SOAT.
> Mr Merrison, this hardly seems rational.
> My company is really extremely small.
> You realise our only product is those little balls
> Of gum you buy in the street out of machines?
> If Corman took me over, I'd understand it.
> But I'm really not cut out for a corporate bandit.
> I've hardly got out from under my last creditor
> And now you're trying to turn me into a predator.

MERRISON.
> The smaller you are, the bigger the triumph for me.
> I can raise four billion dollars of junk.

SOAT.
> Mr Merrison. I'm afraid I'm in a funk.
> I don't know what to say. What're you doin'?

MERRISON.
> I'm using you, Mr Soat, to humiliate
> Somebody I have good reason to hate.

SOAT.
>   I'm not sure –

MERRISON.
>   I wouldn't like to ruin
>   Missouri Gumballs, it seems kind of dumb.

SOAT.
>   No no. No no no no. Don't take my gum.
>   I'll think about it. I've thought about it. Great.

CORMAN, GLEASON, *a Cabinet Minister, in the interval at the National Theatre.*

GLEASON.
>   Enjoying the show?

CORMAN.
>   I'm not watching it.

GLEASON.
>   It's excellent of course, they're not botching it.
>   But after a hard day's work my eyes keep closing.
>   I keep jerking awake when they shout.

CORMAN.
>   It's hard to follow the plot if you keep dozing. /
>   What exactly is this meeting all about?

GLEASON.
>   Yes, Goneril and Reagan and Ophelia –
>   Good of you to come.
>   We have here two conflicting interests.
>   On the one hand it's natural the investor
>   Wants to make all the profit that he can,
>   And institutions' duty to the pensioners
>   Does put the onus on the short-term plan.
>   On the other hand one can't but help mention
>   The problems this creates for industry,
>   Who need longterm research and development
>   In order to create more employment.
>   It's hard to reconcile but we must try.

CORMAN.
>   I totally agree with the CBI.
>   Long term issues mustn't be neglected.
>   The responsibility of management –

GLEASON.
>   We – by which I mean of course the government –
>   Recognise that alas nothing's perfect.
>   That's something you learn in politics.
>   We want to cut the top rate of tax,
>   And profit related pay's a good incentive.
>   But we do think things have gone too far

In the quickprofit shortterm direction.
We wouldn't interfere in a free market.
But we are of course approaching an election.

CORMAN.
Absolutely and I hope to give
More than moral support to the party.
I've always been a staunch Conservative.

GLEASON.
My dear fellow, nobody doubts your loyalty.
That's why I have so little hesitation
In asking this small service to the nation.
Drop your bid. Give up. Leave it alone.

CORMAN.
Out of the question. Sorry. Out of the question.

GLEASON.
I absolutely appreciate the problem –

CORMAN.
Leave me alone will you to do my job.

GLEASON.
I'm sorry, Corman, but I must forbid it.
A takeover like this in the present climate
Makes you, and the City, and us look greedy.
Help us be seen to care about the needy.
Help us to counteract the effect of Tebbit.

CORMAN.
What if I say no?

GLEASON.
I wouldn't like to dwell on the unsavoury
Story of that young man's suicide –

CORMAN.
Are you threatening me?

GLEASON.
                              I do admire your bravery.
No, but my colleagues in the DTI
Did, I believe, call on you today.

CORMAN.
Leave it out, Gleason, I've had enough.
DTI? I'm going to call your bluff.
If my takeover's going to hurt your image
Another scandal would do far more damage

GLEASON.
Mr Corman, I'll be brutally frank.
A scandal would not be welcomed by the Bank
Nor will it be tolerated by the Tories.
Whenever you businessmen do something shitty
Some of it gets wiped off on the City,
And the government's smelly from the nasty stories.

Meanwhile, 'Ladies and gentlemen take your seats' etc.

CORMAN.
Us businessmen? / The banks are full of crap.

GLEASON.
So if you persist and make a nasty mess
Not a single bank will handle your business.

CORMAN.
You can't do that, Gleason, don't make me laugh.

GLEASON.
Corman, please, don't make my patience snap.
I wouldn't want to miss the second half.
You drop the bid. We stop the DTI.

CORMAN.
You'd stop the scandal breaking anyway.
Are you telling me you can't control the press?

GLEASON.
Yes, but we'd break you. Do you want to try?
You drop the bid. We stop the DTI.

CORMAN.
Why pick on me? Everyone's the same.
I'm just good at playing a rough game.

GLEASON.
Exactly, and the game must be protected.
You can go on playing after we're elected.
Five more glorious years free enterprise,
And your services to industry will be recognised.

GLEASON *goes.*

CORMAN.
Cunt. Right. Good.
At least a knighthood.

ZAC *and* JACINTA, *exhausted, in the foyer of the Savoy.*

ZAC.
So he cancelled the deal.

JACINTA.
And how do you feel?

ZAC.
Exhausted.

JACINTA.
          I get you a drink.
At least we can meet,
You're not rushed off your feet,
It's better like this I think.

ZAC.

Jacinta, I still can't forgive you for going to Biddulph, the whole deal could have been wrecked.

JACINTA.

But I get more money that way, Zac, really what do you expect?
I can't do bad business just because I feel romantic.

ZAC.

The way you do business, Jacinta, drives me completely frantic.

JACINTA.

I love the way you are so obsessed when you're thinking about your bids.

ZAC.

I love that terrible hospital scam / and the drug addicted kids.

JACINTA.

(That's true, Zac!)
I love the way you never stop work, I hate a man who's lazy.

ZAC.

The way you unloaded your copper mines drove me completely crazy.

JACINTA.

Zac, you're so charming. I'm almost as fond
Of you as I am of a eurobond.

ZAC

I thought we'd never manage to make a date.
You're more of a thrill than a changing interest rate.

JACINTA.

This is a very public place to meet.

ZAC.

Maybe we ought to go up to your suite.

They get up to go.

ZAC.

Did you ever play with a hoop when you were a child and when it stops turning it falls down flat?
I feel kind of like that.

JACINTA.

I am very happy. My feeling for you is deep.
But will you mind very much if we go to sleep?

GREVILLE, *drunk.*

GREVILLE.

Maybe I should retire while my career is at its pinnacle.
Working in the City can make one rather cynical.
When a oil tanker sank with a hundred men the lads cheered because they'd make a million.
When Sadat was shot I was rather chuffed because I was long of gold bullion.

Life's been very good to me. I think I'll work for Oxfam.

FROSBY, *with a gun.*

FROSBY.
    I thought the sun would never set.
    I thought I'd be extremely rich.
    You can't be certain what you'll get.
    I've heard the young say Life's a bitch.

    I betrayed my oldest friend.
    It didn't give me too much fun.
    My way of life is at an end.
    At least I have a friendly gun.

    My word is my junk bond.

DAVE *and* MARTIN *have just come out of a Chinese restaurant. Late night.*

DAVE.
    I've eaten too many crab claws.

MARTIN.
    You'll be sick in the cab again.

DAVE.
    You'll get stick from your wife again.

MARTIN.
    She don't care if I'm late.

DAVE.
    What's she up to then?

MARTIN.
    Watch it.

DAVE.
    Late city, no pity.

BRIAN, TERRY *and* VINCE *follow.*

BRIAN.
    Guy meets a guy and he says what do you do for a living and he says I hurt people. /

TERRY.
    Sounds like my girlfriend.

BRIAN.
    He says you hurt people, he says yes I hurt people for money. / *I'm a hitman.

TERRY.
    Sounds like a trader

MARTIN.
    How much was it?

DAVE.
    Bet it was two fifty.

MARTIN.
Bet it was three hundred.

DAVE.
How much?

MARTIN.
Ten.

VINCE.
Two eighty five.

MARTIN.
Told you. All that crab.

DAVE *gives* MARTIN *ten pounds.*

BRIAN.
*Break a leg, five hundred pounds, break a back, a thousand /

DAVE.
I know him, he works for Liffe.

BRIAN.
And he says I'm glad I met you because my neighbour's carrying on with my wife.
So he takes him home and says see that lighted window, that's where they are, I want her dead,
How much would it cost to shoot her through the head? *

TERRY.
You can't get rid of your money in Crete.
Hire every speedboat, drink till you pass out, eat
Till you puke and you're still loaded with drachs.

MARTIN. ⎫
DAVE.   ⎬   Drach attack! drach attack!
          ⎭

VINCE.
Why's a clitoris like a filofax?

DAVE and OTHERS.
Every cunt's got one.

BRIAN.
*And he says five grand.
And he says, now my neighbour what would it cost if you shot off his prick and his balls.
And he says that's five grand and all.
So he says ten grand! Yes all right, it's worth it, go on, so the hitman's stood there by the garden gate
And he points his gun at the window, and he's stood there and stood there, and he says get on with it, and the hitman says Wait.
Time it right / and I'll save you five grand.

DAVE.
I'll save you five grand.

MARTIN.
Two eurobond dealers walking through Trafalgar Square, one of them said what would you do if a bird shat on your head?
And he said /
I don't think I'd ask her out again.

DAVE.
    I don't think I'd ask her out again.

SCILLA *at* MARYLOU BAINES' *office in New York.*
SCILLA, TK.

TK.
    Hi, I'm TK, Marylou Baines' personal assistant.

SCILLA.
    Tell Marylou Baines
    I've just flown in from London, I've come here straight off the plane.
    I'm Jake Todd's sister and I've got some information
    That I didn't want to trust to the telephone so I've brought it myself personally to its
        destination.

TK.
    Ms Baines won't see you I'm afraid but if you'd like to give me the information instead,
    I'm setting up in business myself and can guarantee you'd receive service second to
        none because it's always those who are starting up who work hardest because they
        want to get ahead.
    So can I help you?

SCILLA.
    I didn't spend six hours crossing the Atlantic
    To be fobbed off by a personal assistant.

TK.
    I'm sorry about this but it is part of my job description to be resistant.

SCILLA.
    I warn you, I'm very tired and I'm getting frantic,
    And Marylou will get a terrible fright
    Tomorrow morning if she doesn't see me tonight.

TK.
    If you just give me some indication of what your problem's about –

SCILLA.
    Get out of my way. OUT OUT OUT.

    MARYLOU *comes in.*

MARYLOU.
    So. Todd's sister. You've come flying
    From London with information?

SCILLA.
                        No, I was lying.
    You don't get information this time, Marylou.
    I want to know things from you.

MARYLOU.
    You can ask.

SCILLA.
I had been wondering if you killed Jake, but now I hardly care.
It's not going to bring him alive again, and the main thing's to get my share.
They left me out because I'm a girl and it's terribly unfair.
You were Jake's main employer so tell me please
How did you pay him his enormous fees?
Did somebody pass a briefcase of notes at a station under a clock?
Or did you make over a whole lot of stock?
Did he have a company and what's its name?
And how can I get in on the game?
You'll need a replacement in London who knows their way round the businesses and
banks.
Can I suggest somebody?

MARYLOU.
No thanks.

SCILLA.
If you don't help me I'll go to the authorities and tell them –

MARYLOU.
Is this blackmail?

SCILLA.
Yes, of course. I can put you in jail.

MARYLOU.
I'll take the risk. I'm a risk arbitrageur.
So run off home.

TK.
And nobody in America runs better risks than her.

SCILLA.
You can stick your arbitrage up your arse.
If you don't tell me about his company
You'll find me quite a dangerous enemy.
I'm greedy and completely amoral.
I've the cunning and connections of the middle class
And I'm tough as a yob.

MARYLOU.
Scilla, don't let's quarrel.
My personal assistant's leaving. Do you want a job?

TK.
Right now?

MARYLOU.
Sure, TK, you said you wanted out,
Scilla wants in. So don't let's hang about.

MARYLOU *and* SCILLA *go.*

TK.
One thing I've learned from working for Marylou:
Do others before they can do you.

ZAC.

ZAC.

So Scilla never came back.

She sent me a postcard of the Statue of Liberty saying Bye bye Zac.

She never did find out who killed her brother but I'm sure it wasn't Corman or Jacinta or Marylou or any of us.

Who didn't want Jake to talk to the DTI? Who wanted him out of the way?

The British government, because another scandal just before the election would have been too much fuss.

So I reckon it was MI5 or the CIA.

(Or he could even have shot himself, the kid wasn't stable.)

There's bound to be endless scandals in the city but really it's incidental.

It can be a nuisance because it gives the wrong impression

And if people lose confidence in us there could be a big recession.

Sure this is a dangerous system and it could crash any minute and I sometimes wake up in bed

And think is Armageddon Aids, nuclear war or a crash, and how will I end up dead?
(But that's just before breakfast.)

What really matters is the massive sums of money being passed round the world, and trying to appreciate their size can drive you mental.

There haven't been a million days since Christ died.

So think a billion, that's a thousand million, and have you ever tried

To think a trillion? Think a trillion dollars a day.

That's the gross national product of the USA.

There's people who say the American eagle is more like a vulture.

I say don't piss on your own culture.

Naturally there's a whole lot of greed and

That's no problem because money buys freedom.

So the Tories kept the scandal to the minimum. Greville Todd was arrested and put in prison to show the government was serious about keeping the city clean and nobody shed any tears.

And the Conservatives romped home with a landslide victory for five more glorious years.
(Which was handy though not essential because it would take far more than Labour to stop us.)

I've been having a great time raising sixteen billion dollars to build a satellite,
And I reckon I can wrap it up tonight.

EVERYBODY

SCILLA.

Scilla's been named by Business Week as Wall Street's rising star.

GREVILLE.

Greville walked out of the open prison but didn't get very far.

GRIMES.

Grimes does insider dealing for Scilla and Marylou (and he bought Greville's house).

JAKE.

Jake's ghost appeared to Jacinta one midnight in Peru.

JACINTA.
> Jacinta marries Zac next week and they honeymoon in Shanghai.
>> (Good business to be done in China now.)

NIGEL.
> Nigel Ajibala's doing something in Dubai.

CORMAN.
> Lord Corman's helping organise the tunnel under the channel.
>> (He's also chairman of the board of the National Theatre.)

ETHERINGTON.
> Etherington runs the City's new disciplinary panel.

DUCKETT.
> Duckett had a breakdown and was given ECT.

BIDDULPH.
> Biddulph's running Albion and is big in ITV.

TK.
> TK ended up in jail because of some funny tricks.

MARYLOU.
> Marylou Baines ran for president in 1996.

MERRISON.
> Merrison's been ambassador to London, Paris, Rome.

DURKFELD.
> Durkfeld had a heart attack one quiet Sunday at home.

SOAT.
> Soat acquired Corman Enterprise and a dangerous reputation.

STARR.
> Dolcie Starr does his PR so he's loved by the whole nation.

TERRY.
> Terry went to Chicago and did a lot of coke.

VINCE.
> Vince spent every penny he earned and thought it was a joke.

KATHY.
> Kathy's got a telly spot, advice on buying shares.

JOANNE.
> Joanne became a trader and soon she moved upstairs.

MARTIN.
> Martin moved to eurobonds.

BRIAN.
> Brian bought a deer park.

DAVE.
> Dave went to Australia and was eaten by a shark.

FROSBY.
> Frosby was forgotten.

FIVE MORE GLORIOUS YEARS

Wa-doooo do-ya-doody, wa-doooo do-ya-do
These are the best years of our lives, let wealth and favour be our guide
We can expect another five, join hands across the great divide
BACKUP: wa-doooo do-ya-doody, wa-doooo do-ya-doody
            Say-wa   do-ya-doody, wa-doooo do-ya-do

So raise your oysters and champagne, and as we toast the blushing bride
Pon crystal mountains of cocaine, our nostrils flare and open wide
B/U: tippy-tum-tee-tippy-tum-tum, tippy-tippy tum-tum
        tippy-tum-tee-tippy-tum-tum, tippy-tippy tum-tum
        say-wa   tippy-tippy tum-tum
        tippy-tum-tee-tippy-tum-tum, tippy-tippy tum-tum

Chorus:
Five more glorious years, five more glorious years
B/U: we're saved from the valley of tears for five more glorious years
        pissed and promiscuous the money's ridiculous
        send her victorious for five fucking morious
        Five more glorious years

These are the best years of our lives, with information from inside
My new Ferrari has just arrived, these pleasures stay unqualified
B/U: Fiddle diddle iddle fiddle diddle, fiddle diddle iddle
        Fiddle diddle iddle fiddle diddle, fiddle diddle iddle
        Say-wa   fiddle diddle iddle
        Fiddle-diddle-iddle-fiddle-diddle-fiddle-diddle-iddle

Chorus:
Five more glorious years, five more glorious years
B/U: we're crossing forbidden frontiers, we're sniding beneath our veneer
        pissed and promiscuous, the money's ridiculous
        send her victorious for five fucking morious
        five more glorious years
Five more glorious years, five more glorious years
        we're saved from the valley of tears for five more glorious years
        pissed and promiscuous, the money's ridiculous
        send her victorious for five fucking morious
        five more glorious years

A capella:
These are the best years of our lives, these are the best years of our lives
These are the best years of our lives, these are the best years of our lives
B/U: wa-doooo do-ya-doody, wa-doooo do-ya-doody
        Say-wa   do-ya-doody, wa-doooo do-ya-do

These are the best years of our lives, and as we toast the blushing bride
My maserati has arrived, join hands across the great divide
B/U: fiddle diddle iddle fiddle diddle, fiddle diddle iddle
        fiddle diddle iddle fiddle diddle, fiddle diddle iddle
        Say-wa   fiddle diddle iddle
        Fiddle diddle iddle- ddle diddle, fiddle diddle iddle

Chorus:
Five more glorious years, five more glorious years
B/U: we're saved from the valley of tears for five more glorious years
      pissed and promiscuous, the money's ridiculous
      send her victorious for five fucking morious
      five more glorious years

Chorus:
Five more glorious years, five more glorious years
B/U: We're crossing forbidden frontiers for five more glorious years
      pissed and promiscuous, the money's ridiculous
      send her victorious for five fucking morious
      five more glorious years